CONTEÚDO DIGITAL PARA ALUNOS

Cadastre-se e transforme seus estudos em uma experiência única de aprendizado:

Entre na página de cadastro:
https://sistemas.editoradobrasil.com.br/cadastro

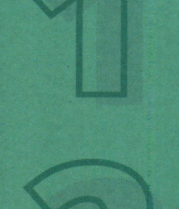

Além dos seus dados pessoais e dos dados de sua escola, adicione ao cadastro o código do aluno, que garantirá a exclusividade do seu ingresso à plataforma.

1121910A8367427

Depois, acesse:
https://leb.editoradobrasil.com.br/
e navegue pelos conteúdos digitais de sua coleção **:D**

Lembre-se de que esse código, pessoal e intransferível, é valido por um ano. Guarde-o com cuidado, pois é a única maneira de você acessar os conteúdos da plataforma.

ENSINO FUNDAMENTAL ANOS INICIAIS

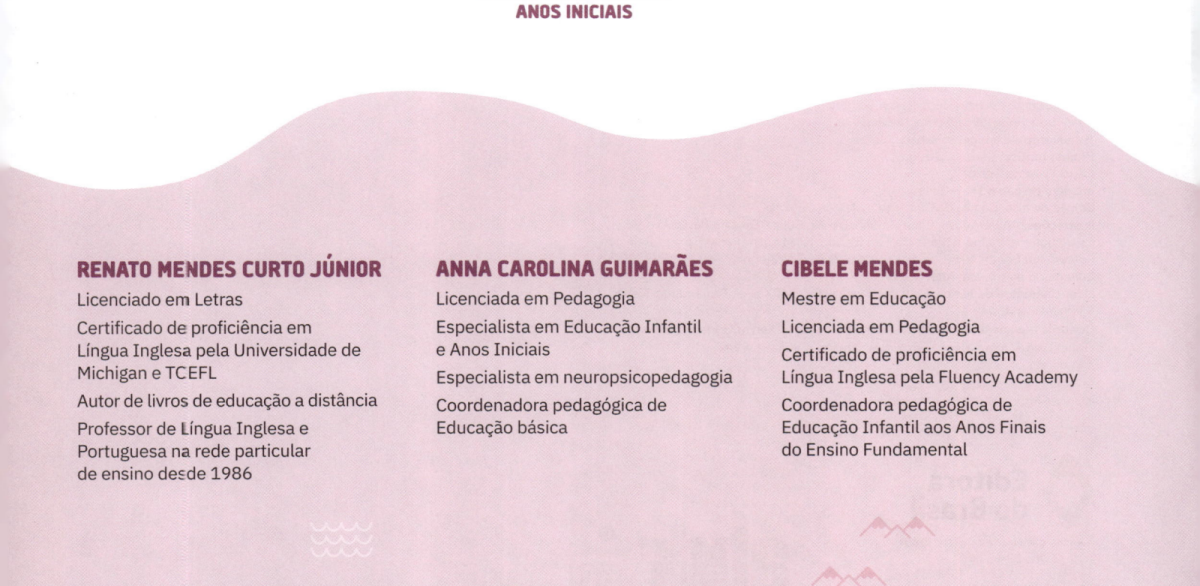

RENATO MENDES CURTO JÚNIOR

Licenciado em Letras

Certificado de proficiência em Língua Inglesa pela Universidade de Michigan e TCEFL

Autor de livros de educação a distância

Professor de Língua Inglesa e Portuguesa na rede particular de ensino desde 1986

ANNA CAROLINA GUIMARÃES

Licenciada em Pedagogia

Especialista em Educação Infantil e Anos Iniciais

Especialista em neuropsicopedagogia

Coordenadora pedagógica de Educação básica

CIBELE MENDES

Mestre em Educação

Licenciada em Pedagogia

Certificado de proficiência em Língua Inglesa pela Fluency Academy

Coordenadora pedagógica de Educação Infantil aos Anos Finais do Ensino Fundamental

 **Editora do Brasil**

Dados Internacionais de Catalogação na Publicação (CIP)
(Câmara Brasileira do Livro, SP, Brasil)

Curto Júnior, Renato Mendes
Brincando com inglês 4 : ensino fundamental:
anos iniciais / Renato Mendes Curto Júnior, Anna
Carolina Guimarães, Cibele Mendes. -- 5. ed. --
São Paulo : Editora do Brasil, 2024. -- (Brincando
com)

ISBN 978-85-10-09496-2 (aluno)
ISBN 978-85-10-09497-9 (professor)

1. Língua inglesa (Ensino fundamental)
I. Guimarães, Anna Carolina. II. Mendes, Cibele.
III. Título. IV. Série.

24-196548	CDD-372.652

Índices para catálogo sistemático:

1. Língua inglesa : Ensino fundamental 372.652
Cibele Maria Dias - Bibliotecária - CRB-8/9427

© Editora do Brasil S.A., 2024
Todos os direitos reservados

Direção-geral: Paulo Serino de Souza

Diretoria editorial: Felipe Ramos Poletti
Gerência editorial de conteúdo didático: Erika Caldin
Gerência editorial de produção e design: Ulisses Pires
Supervisão de design: Dea Melo
Supervisão de arte: Abdonildo José de Lima Santos
Supervisão de revisão: Elaine Cristina da Silva
Supervisão de iconografia: Léo Burgos
Supervisão de digital: Priscila Hernandez
Supervisão de controle e planejamento editorial: Roseli Said
Supervisão de direitos autorais: Jennifer Xavier

Supervisão editorial: Carla Felix Lopes e Diego Mata
Edição: Danuza D. Gonçalves, Graziele Arantes Mattiuzzi, Natália Feulo, Nayra Simões e Sheila Fabre
Assistência editorial: Igor Gonçalves, Julia do Nascimento, Natalia Soeda e Pedro Andrade Bezerra
Revisão: 2014 Soluções Editoriais, Alexander Siqueira, Andréia Andrade, Beatriz Dorini, Gabriel Ornelas, Jonathan Busato, Júlia Castelo Branco, Mariana Paixão, Martin Gonçalves, Rita Costa, Rosani Andreani e Sandra Fernandes
Pesquisa iconográfica: Selma Nagano
Tratamento de imagens: Robson Mereu
Projeto gráfico: Caronte Design
Capa: Caronte Design
Imagem de capa: Thais Castro
Edição de arte: Camila de Camargo e Marcos Gubiotti
Ilustrações: André Aguiar, Clara Gavilan, Danillo Souza, Dayane Raven, Desenhorama, Evandro Marenda, Lais Bicudo, Luiz Lentini, Paulo Borges, Reinaldo Rosa, Valter Ferrari, Vanessa Alexandre e Vinicius Meneghin
Editoração eletrônica: Abel Design
Licenciamentos de textos: Cinthya Utiyama, Jennifer Xavier, Paula Harue Tozaki e Renata Garbellini
Controle e planejamento editorial: Ana Fernandes, Bianca Gomes, Juliana Gonçalves, Maria Trofino, Terezinha Oliveira e Valéria Alves

5ª edição / 1ª impressão, 2024
Impresso na Hawaii Gráfica e Editora

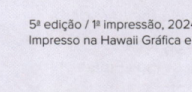

Avenida das Nações Unidas, 12901
Torre Oeste, 20º andar
São Paulo, SP – CEP: 04578-910
Fone: + 55 11 3226-0211
www.editoradobrasil.com.br

Respeite o direito autoral

APRESENTAÇÃO

Querido aluno, querida aluna,

Este material foi elaborado para que você aprenda inglês de forma divertida, por meio de atividades estimulantes e desafiadoras, com o intuito de transformar a sala de aula em um espaço para praticar a língua inglesa brincando!

Nesta nova versão do **Brincando com Inglês**, cada aula será uma nova experiência, e você não vai querer parar de aprender. Vamos começar?

Os autores

CONHEÇA SEU LIVRO

Boas-vindas à nova edição do **Brincando com Inglês**!

LET'S START!
No início de cada volume, esta seção resgata conhecimentos prévios e apresenta atividades lúdicas que possibilitam a preparação para os novos conteúdos.

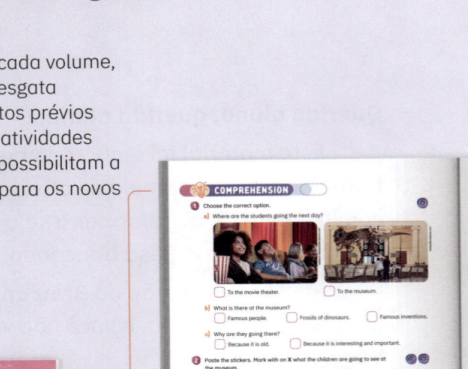

VOCABULARY
Apresenta o vocabulário das palavras vistas na unidade, com a tradução em língua portuguesa.

COMPREHENSION
As atividades desta seção visam à compreensão do texto visto na abertura da unidade.

LET'S LISTEN
Seção com atividades que têm como objetivo a compreensão de áudios.

GOOD DEED
Apresenta atividades temáticas de cunho social e ético relacionadas ao assunto de cada unidade. Aborda as competências gerais e socioemocionais da BNCC e as atividades feitas em grupo ou em dupla.

LET'S SING!

Músicas para os alunos cantarem e praticarem o vocabulário visto na unidade de forma lúdica e divertida.

LITERARY TIME

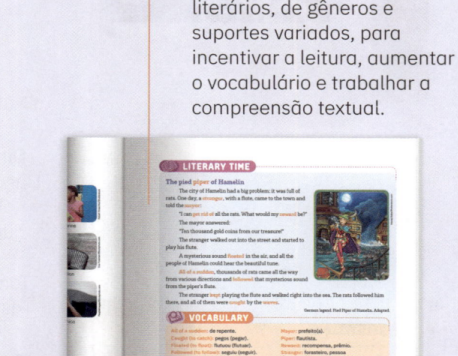

Boxe com pequenos textos literários, de gêneros e suportes variados, para incentivar a leitura, aumentar o vocabulário e trabalhar a compreensão textual.

GRAMMAR POINT

Boxe com conteúdos gramaticais para que você compreenda a estrutura estudada e sistematize escrita e oralidade.

LET'S PLAY

Seção relacionada aos conceitos propostos e à temática da unidade. Você encontrará atividades lúdicas, como diagrama de palavras, jogos de relacionar, jogos de erros, desafios etc.

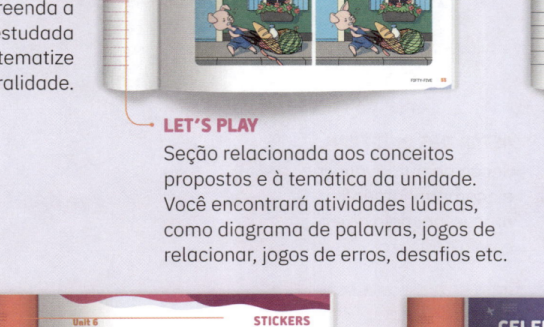

STICKERS

Adesivos para colar em algumas atividades.

CELEBRATIONS

Encartes com atividades relacionadas a datas comemorativas.

DIGITAL PLAY

Seção que trabalha atividades com uso de tecnologia: filmagem, fotos, uso de apps e jogos *on-line*.

ENGLISH AROUND THE WORLD

Seção que contempla a Dimensão Intercultural da Língua Inglesa, trabalhando elementos da cultura em que se fala o idioma como língua oficial ou franca. Também são estudados os aspectos interculturais de outros países.

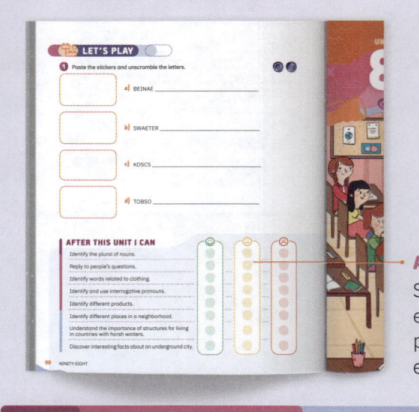

AFTER THIS UNIT I CAN...

Seção de autoavaliação e acompanhamento processual pelo aluno e pelo professor.

ÍCONES

ADESIVO	COLAR	FALAR OU CONVERSAR
APONTAR	COLORIR	LIGAR/RELACIONAR
CANTAR	CONTAR	MARCAR
CARTONADO	DESENHAR	RECORTAR
CIRCULAR	ENCONTRAR/PESQUISAR	TRAÇAR/ESCREVER

CONTENTS

LET'S START! _____ **8**

UNIT 1
A special school day _____ **17**

UNIT 2
Sports and health _____ **29**

UNIT 3
A friend's visit _____ **39**

UNIT 4
At the cafeteria _____ **51**

UNIT 5
The fun visit to the museum _____ **63**

UNIT 6
The music class _____ **75**

UNIT 7
At the shopping mall _____ **89**

UNIT 8
Different jobs _____ **99**

REVIEW _____ **109**

GLOSSARY _____ **121**

INDEX

SONGS _____ **127**

LISTENINGS _____ **127**

CELEBRATIONS _____ **129**

STICKERS _____ **145**

LET'S START!

1 Find the names of the colors in the wordsearch.

Y	T	O	O	U	N	A	F	G
S	E	F	R	I	S	O	W	H
W	H	L	E	R	K	R	H	K
X	U	S	L	I	L	A	I	I
C	A	B	R	O	W	N	T	O
G	R	X	P	I	W	G	E	F
O	P	R	M	U	L	E	Y	D
G	R	E	E	N	A	X	J	V
P	Y	D	U	B	L	L	C	B
U	E	W	K	A	Y	F	Y	L
B	L	A	C	K	E	K	G	U
A	E	K	P	U	R	P	L	E
P	I	N	K	N	J	H	G	T

Black
Blue
Brown
Green
Orange
Pink
Purple
Red
White
Yellow

Draw your teacher and write his/her name.

My teacher's name is _____

3 What are they? Match the word with the corresponding picture.

a) desk

b) board

c) wastebasket

d) window

e) fan

f) bookshelf

4 **Circle the corresponding number.**

a) Eleven candies.

b) Fifteen lollipops.

c) Eighteen cupcakes.

d) Ten popsicles.

5 **Answer the questions.**

a) What is your name?

___

b) What is your friend's name?

___

6 Complete the crossword with wild animals.

7 Color your favorite farm animal.

8 Color the picture accordingly. Then write the corresponding words.

1) brown – _____

2) blue – _____

3) yellow – _____

4) pink – _____

5) black – _____

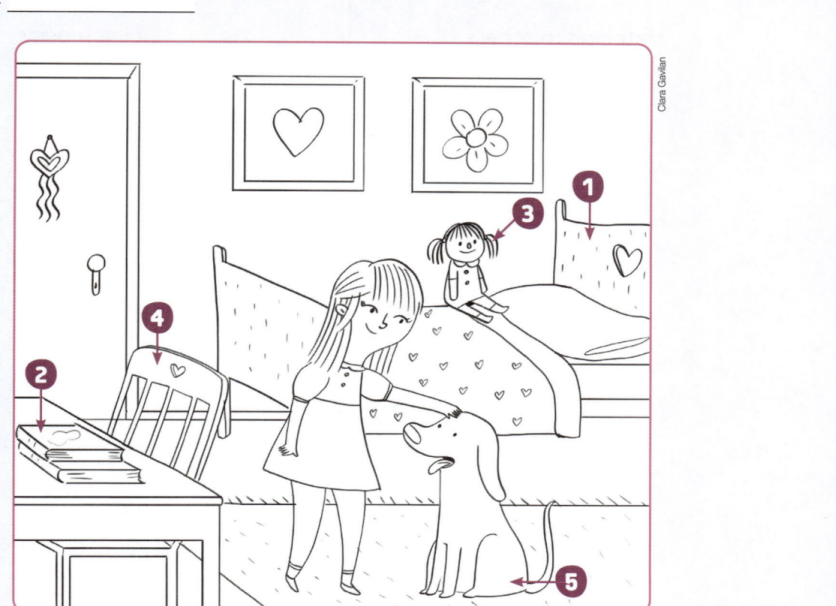

9 Choose five musical instruments, circle them, and write their names.

_____

_____

10 Color the pictures that represent good choices.

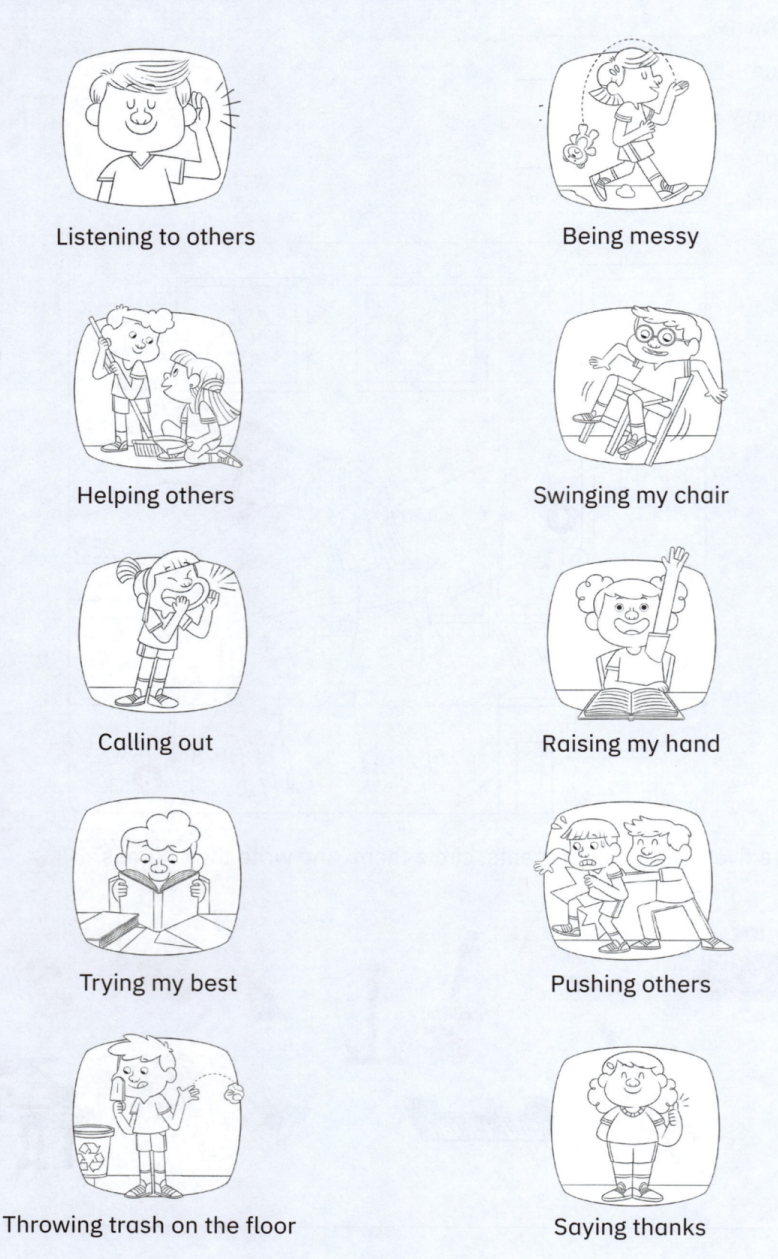

11 What are the names of these places? Paste the stickers.

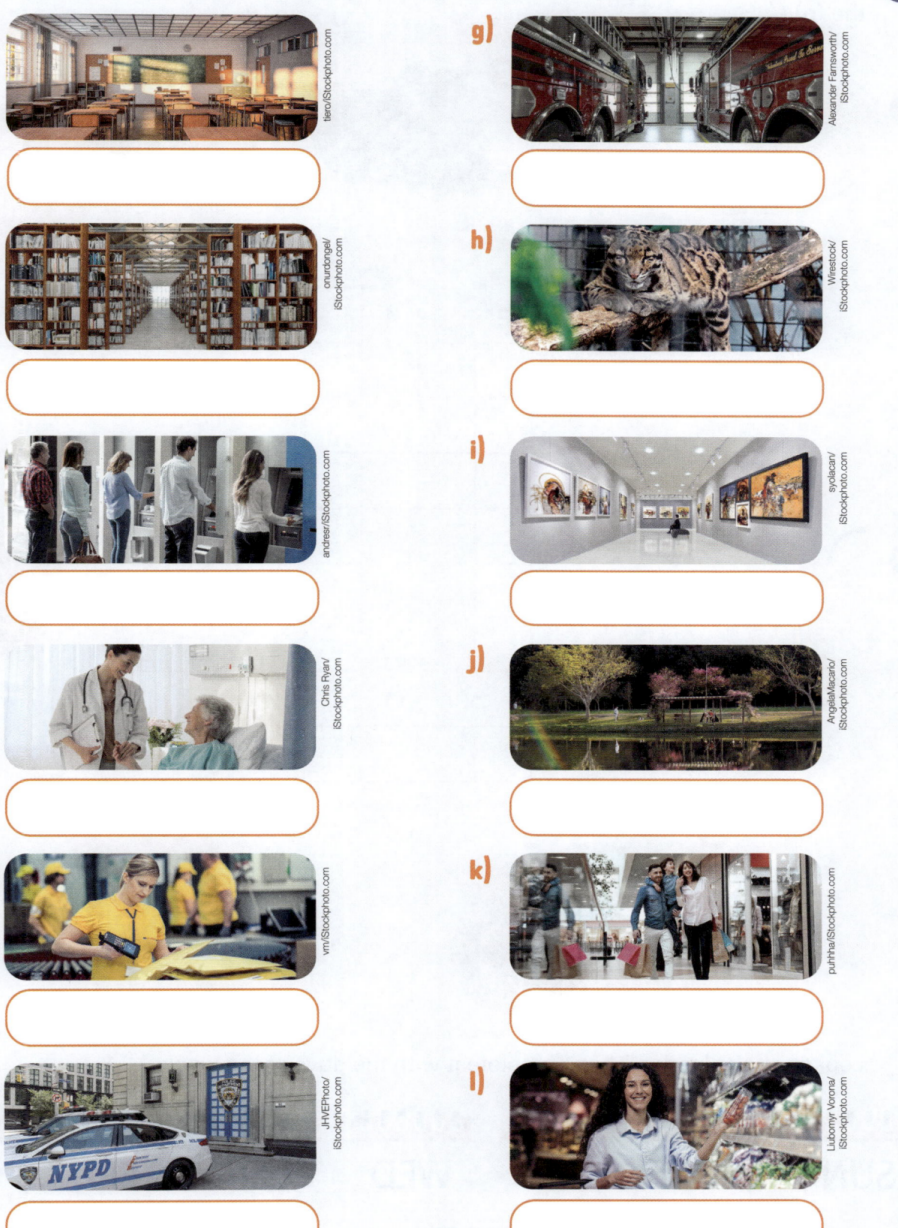

12 Observe the pictures. Then complete the crossword puzzle with the name of the fruit.

13 Look at the calendar. Then complete it with the days of the week.

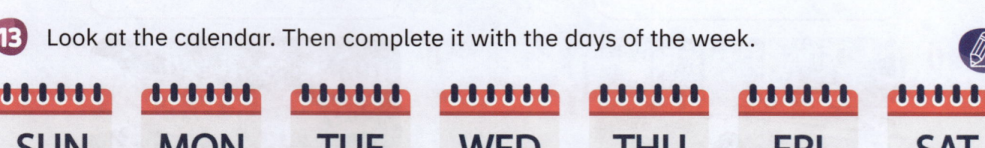

| Sunday | Monday | _____ | _____ | Thursday | _____ | _____ |

UNIT 1 A SPECIAL SCHOOL DAY

 VOCABULARY

Beginning: começo.
Class: aula.
Excited for: animado(a) para.
Football: futebol americano.
My favorite: minha favorita/meu favorito.
Physical Education: Educação Física.
Wait (to wait): esperar.
What's up?: E aí?

COMPREHENSION

1 **Answer the questions.**

a) Why are the students so excited? Who are they waiting for?

___

___

b) What is Jeremy's favorite class?

___

c) What is Jonas's favorite class?

___

2 **Do the students know each other? Mark X on the correct answer.**

☐ Yes.

☐ No.

3 **Mark your three favorite school subjects.**

a) Science ☐

b) History ☐

c) Geography ☐

d) Physical Education ☐

e) English ☐

f) Art ☐

g) Portuguese ☐

h) Math ☐

1 Complete the school timetable according to the color code.

	Monday	**Tuesday**	**Wednesday**	**Thursday**	**Friday**
7:15	History	English	Portuguese	History	Math
8:05	Portuguese	Science	Portuguese	English	Math
8:45	English	Art	Portuguese	English	Art
9:55	Science	Math	Physical Education	English	Physical Education
10:45	Science	Math	Physical Education	Portuguese	Art

🟡 Math 🔴 English 🟠 Portuguese 🟢 Science

🟣 History 🩷 Geography 🔵 Physical Education 🔴 Art

A_B^C GRAMMAR POINT

Prepositions of place

At	**In**	**On**
Specific place	**Closed space**	**Surface**
at the corner	in a car	on the wall
at the bus stop	in the house	on a page
at the door	in a box	on the floor

Near	**In front of**	**Between**
Close, at a short distance	**Near and in the face of something**	**In the middle of two things**
near the school	in front of the desk	between two dogs
near the book	in front of the man	between two desks
near the shelves	in front of the shop	between two cars

GOOD DEED

Welcome to school!

Write a welcome message to a new colleague.

LET'S LISTEN

1 Listen to the sentences. Then observe the picture and complete them.

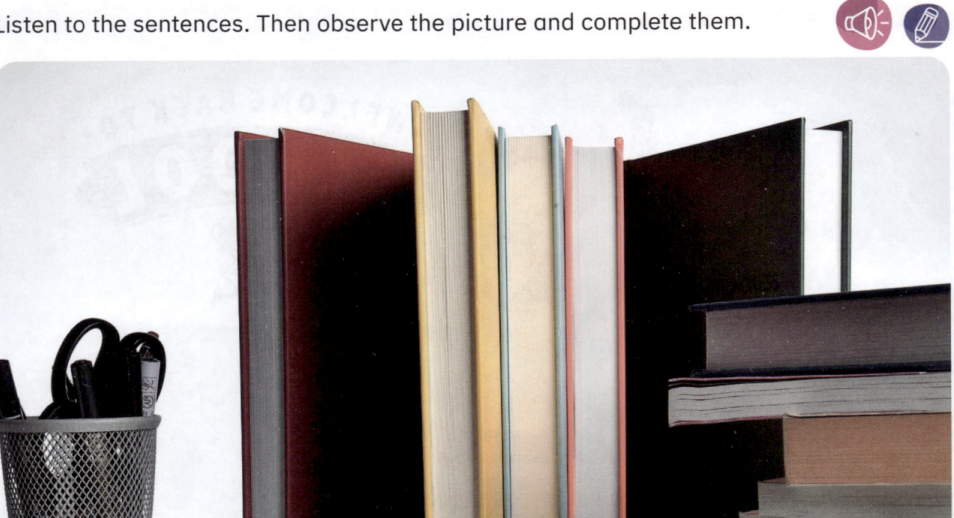

a) There is a yellow book _____ the red book and the blue book.

b) The glasses are _____ five books.

c) The books are _____ the pen holder.

d) There are a few pens _____ the pen holder.

e) The glasses are _____ the table.

f) Those things are _____ the office.

g) There are thirteen books _____ the table.

DIGITAL PLAY

Sustainable shopping in the United States

What is the solution to the problem of shopping for people around the world? Check the appropriate answer.

☐ Consumerism.

☐ Sustainable shopping.

ENGLISH AROUND THE WORLD

Discover the Great Britain

Circle the largest and smallest country on the United Kingdom map.

Work and play

LET'S SING!

Here at school, we **gather daily**,
and we learn the golden rule.
Still aspiring, never **tiring**,
that is what we learn at school!

Lessons over, then each rover
laughs the happy hours away.
Merry **playmates**, **blithe** and happy **mates**,
that's the way we do at school!

Work and play, we **mingle** daily,
both we do with loving **zest**.
Never tiring, still aspiring,
till the sun sinks in the west.

Public domain song. Adapted.

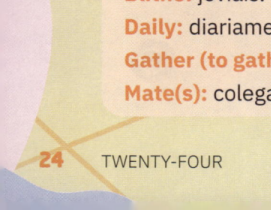

 VOCABULARY

Blithe: joviais.
Daily: diariamente.
Gather (to gather): reunimos (reunir).
Mate(s): colega(s).

Mingle (to mingle): misturamos (misturar).
Playmate(s): colega(s) de brincadeira.
Tiring: cansativo.
Zest: graça.

LITERARY TIME

Let's read a Peanuts comic strip!

1 Do you know Peanuts comic strips? What do you know about them?

___

___

2 What are the characters doing?

___

___

3 What does the dog do in the third panel?

☐ The dog hugs the girl. ☐ The dog kisses the girl.

4 What does smak mean?

☐ A sound of a kiss. ☐ A sound of a music.

5 Observe the end of the story and answer: Did she like the dog's kiss?

___

___

6 Finish the story. Draw the next panel for the comic strip.

GRAMMAR POINT

Indefinite articles

A – consonant sound	An – vowel sound
a house	an apartment
a bedroom	an orange
a garage	an hour

LET'S PLAY

1 Fill in the gaps with the correct articles.

a) _____ cake

b) _____ elephant

c) _____ pencil

d) _____ airplane

e) _____ bear

f) _____ ear

g) _____ friend

h) _____ enemy

LET'S LISTEN

1 Who likes each school subject? Listen and match.

a) Jonas · History

b) Carol · Physical Education

c) Jeremy · Math

d) Thomas · Science

e) M lena · Music

2 Find six school subjects in the wordsearch.

I	A	U	A	O	C	O	U	T	F	H	U	M	O	A
G	L	E	I	G	A	U	D	S	C	I	E	N	C	E
F	H	P	O	R	T	U	G	U	E	S	E	L	U	I
A	G	H	A	U	T	F	A	M	A	T	H	I	C	G
A	R	T	P	T	H	H	E	R	B	O	T	G	F	R
H	A	M	O	C	U	G	E	O	G	R	A	P	H	Y
K	H	E	Y	A	B	O	R	T	I	Y	U	Q	L	M

1 Look at the pictures. Then paste the stickers to complete the sentences.

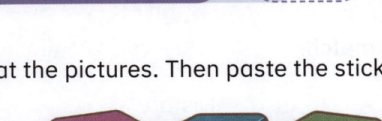

a) Number 3 is _____ number 1 and number 2.

b) The bucket is _____ the shovel.

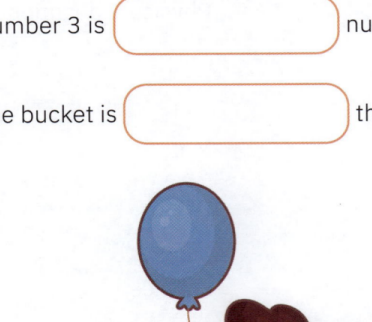

c) The balloon is _____ the boy.

d) The ball is _____ the table.

AFTER THIS UNIT I CAN

Identify prepositions and use them adequately.

Identify school subjects.

Identify the indefinite articles.

Understand the importance of sustainable purchasing and avoiding consumerism.

Identify the formation of the United Kingdom.

COMPREHENSION

1 Do the kids think sports are good for health?

⬜ Yes, they do. ⬜ No, they don't.

2 What sport does Alex like? Which sport is Natasha fan?

___

___

3 Where are they?

___

___

4 Look at the pictures. Use the stickers to name each sport.

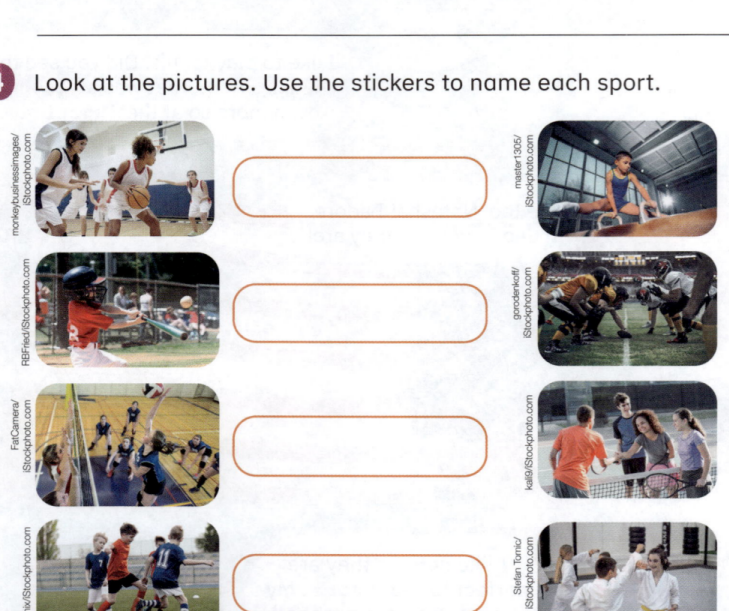

5 Go back to activity 4 and circle the sport presented in the opening scene.

LET'S PLAY

1 Unscramble the letters and name the sports. Then complete the crossword.

a)

llbtaekbas

_____

c)

yellovllab

_____

b)

atskgin

_____

d)

cliycng

_____

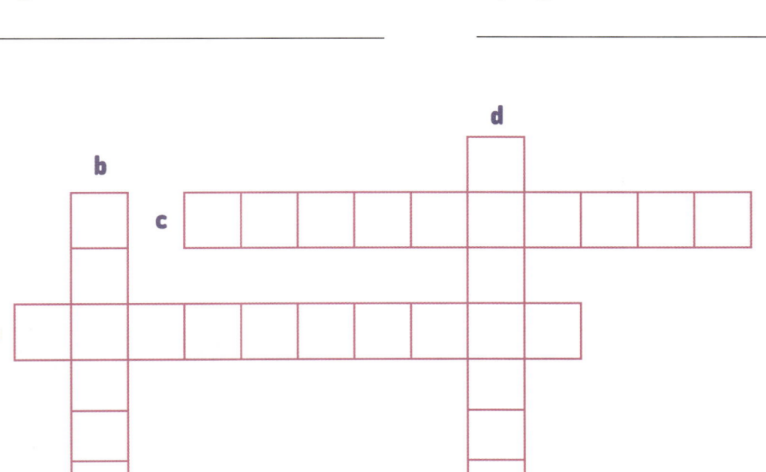

GRAMMAR POINT

Possessive pronouns

A possessive pronoun shows ownership.

This book is **mine.**

Subject pronoun		Possessive pronoun
I		**Mine**
You	**Singular**	**Yours**
He		**His**
She		**Hers**
It (things or animals)		**Its** (things or animals)
We		**Ours**
You	**Plural**	**Yours**
They		**Theirs**

LET'S PLAY

1 Look at the images and complete the sentences with the appropriate possessive pronoun.

a)

This ball is _____.

b)

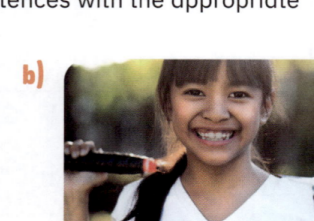

This tennis racket is _____.

GOOD DEED

Sports: everyone can participate!

Research examples of adaptive sports or parasports like the ones in the Paralympic Games.

LET'S LISTEN

1 Listen to the sentences and complete the blank spaces with the appropriate options.

a) You have your swimming goggles, but he doesn't have _____.

b) I cm not sure if this bike is _____ or not.

c) They are pretty sure that the basketball equipment is _____.

LET'S SING!

Take me out to the ball game

Nelly Kelly loved baseball games,
knew the players, knew all their names.
You could see her there every day,
shout "Hurray"!
When they play.
Her **boyfriend** Joe **said**
"To Coney **Isle**, dear, let's go".
Then Nelly started **to fret** and **pout**,
and to him, I **heard** her shout:

Chorus:
Take me **out** to the ball game,
take me out with the **crowd**;
buy me some **peanuts** and Cracker Jacks,
I don't **care** if I never **get back**.
Let me **root**, root, root for the home **team**,
if they don't **win**, it's a **shame**.
For it's one, two, three strikes, you're out,
at the old ball game.

Song by Jack Norworth and Albert Von Tilzer. Unofficial anthem of North America Baseball. Adapted.

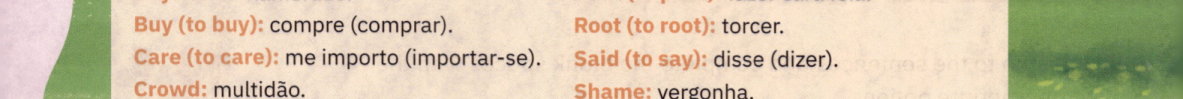

 VOCABULARY

Boyfriend: namorado.	**Pout (to pout):** fazer cara feia.
Buy (to buy): compre (comprar).	**Root (to root):** torcer.
Care (to care): me importo (importar-se).	**Said (to say):** disse (dizer).
Crowd: multidão.	**Shame:** vergonha.
Fret (to fret): incomodar.	**Shout (to shout):** grita (gritar).
Get back: voltar.	**Take me out:** me leve para passear (to take out).
Heard (to hear): ouvi (ouvir).	**Team:** time.
Isle: ilha.	**Win (to win):** vencerem (vencer).
Peanut(s): amendoim(ns).	

DIGITAL PLAY

Discover the flags of English-speaking countries

Identify and write the name of three countries that are represented on the flags.

ENGLISH AROUND THE WORLD

The Olympics and the Winter Olympic Games

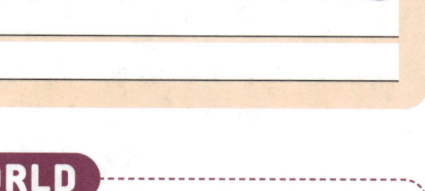

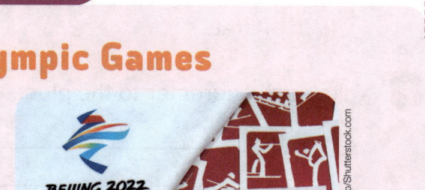

Circle the image which represents the Winter Olympic Games.

1 Listen to the dialogue and answer the questions.

a) Who plays basketball in a wheelchair?

☐ Milena.

☐ Grace.

☐ Henry.

b) When is the next wheelchair basketball match?

☐ Next Wednesday.

☐ Next Thursday.

☐ Next Friday.

c) What sport does Henry play?

☐ Baseball.

☐ Soccer.

☐ Karate.

2 Take each character to the place where they practice sports.

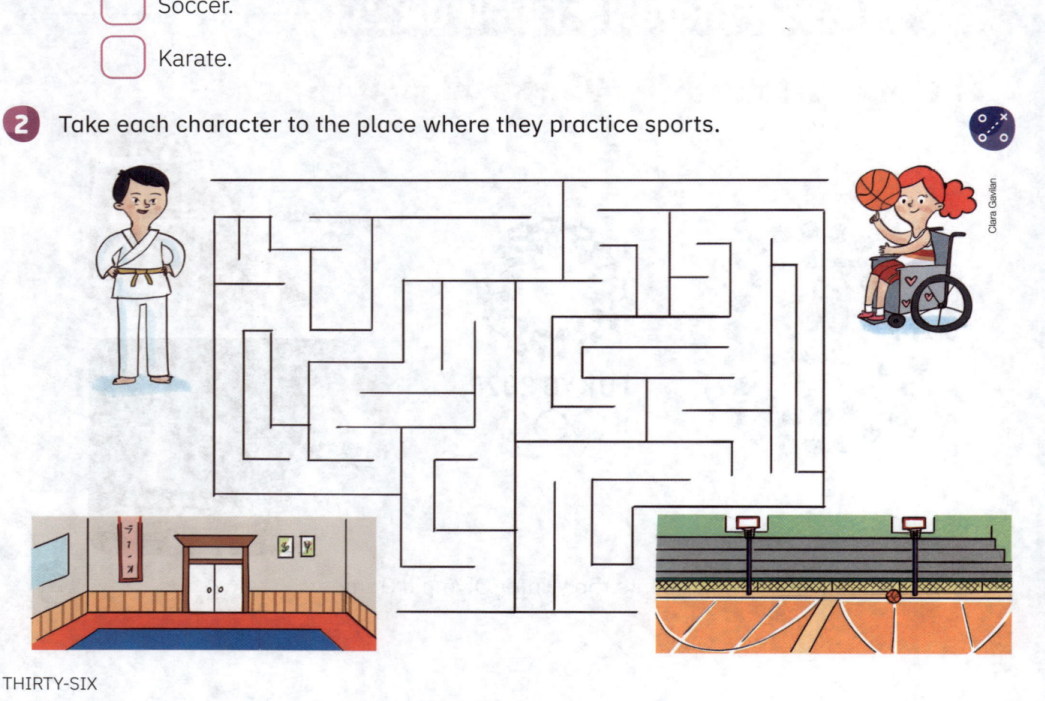

LITERARY TIME

The Hare and the Tortoise

The Hare was once **showing off** his speed before the other animals and **challenged** them:

"I challenge anyone here to race with me."

The Tortoise said quietly:

"I accept your challenge."

The Hare did not believe and made fun of it, but the Tortoise answered:

"Shall we race?"

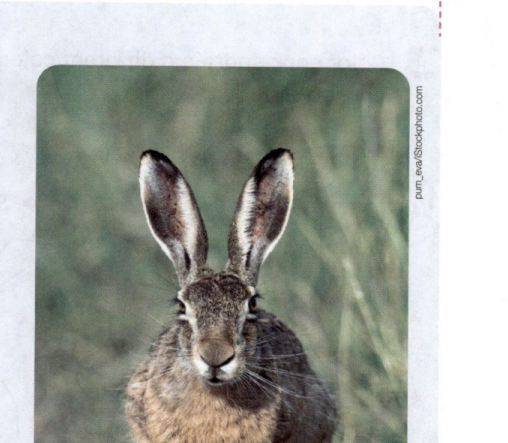

So the race was arranged. The Hare ran fast and was **out of sight** really soon, but he decided to stop and **take a nap**. The Tortoise **plodded on** and plodded on, and when the Hare woke up, he saw the Tortoise winning the race.

After that, the Hare always remembers, "Don't **brag** about your speed, for the slow and steady won the race!."

Aesop fable. Adapted.

VOCABULARY

Brag (to brag): vanglorie-se (vangloriar-se).
Challenged (to challenge): desafiou (desafiar).
Out of sight: longe dos olhos.

Plodded on (to plod on): andou bem devagar (andar bem devagar).
Showing off (to show off): gabando-se (gabar-se).
Take a nap: tirar uma soneca.

1 What was the Hare doing?

- The Hare was hiding her speed.
- The Hare was showing off her speed.

2 What did the Hare do in the middle of the race?

- The Hare took a nap.
- The Hare ran fast.

LET'S PLAY

1 Color each sport in a different color, then paint the respective equipment in the chosen colors.

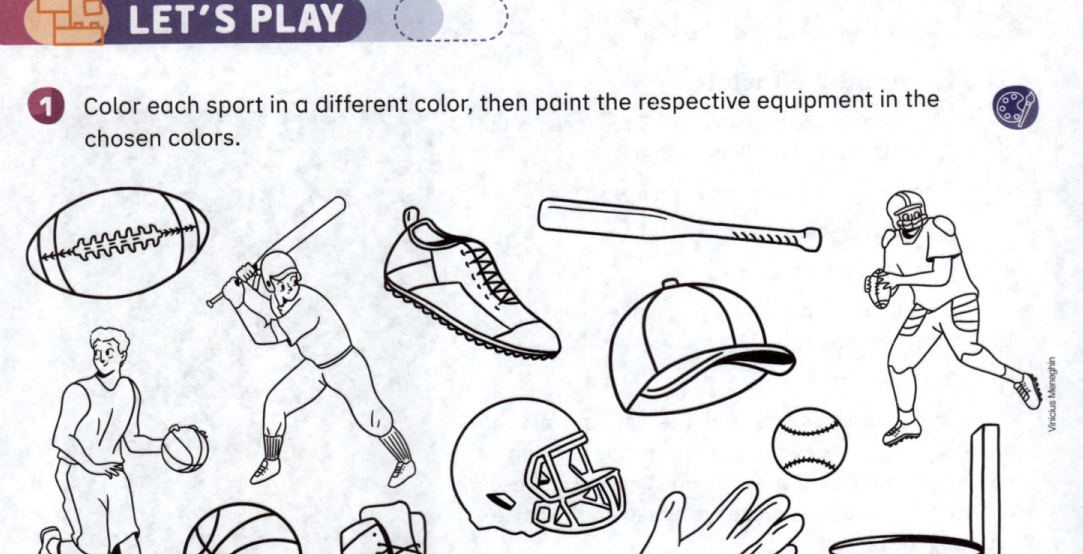

AFTER THIS UNIT I CAN

	😊	😐	😟
Identify possessive pronouns.			
Identify different types of sport.			
Identify and use the verb to be.			
Identify the importance of ethics and respect in the Paralympic Games.			
Recognize some information about the flags of English-speaking countries.			
Recognize some information about the Olympics and Winter Olympic Games.			
Understand words in context by developing vocabulary in English.			

COMPREHENSION

1 Match the columns. What activities does each character want to do?

to play

to watch a movie

to cook

to eat

to talk

2 How long will the visit last?

⬜ One day.

⬜ One morning.

⬜ One night.

⬜ One afternoon.

1 **This** or **that**? Circle the right word according to the character's position.

a) **This/That** is my backpack.

b) **This/That** is my book.

c) **This/That** is my basket ball.

d) **This/That** is my backpack.

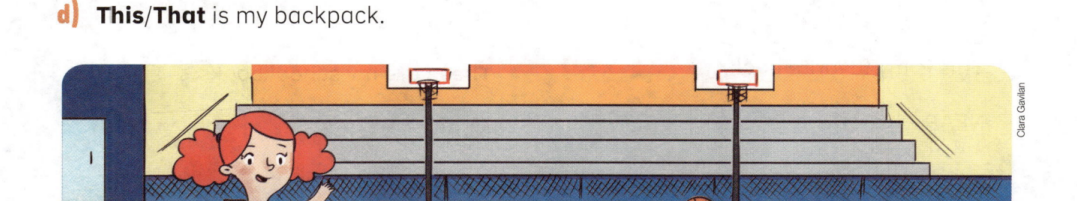

2 Write a sentence using *this* or *that* and draw it.

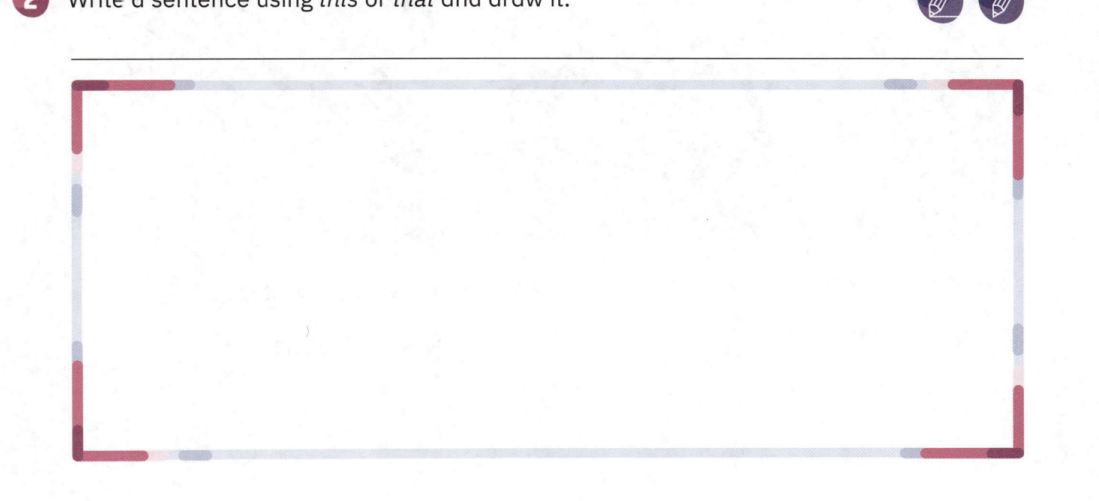

GRAMMAR POINT

Demonstrative pronouns

Demonstrative pronouns are used to point to or indicate a specific person, place, thing or idea.

This is my favorite book.

NEAR → **THIS**

These are my school books.

NEAR → **THESE**

That is my bike.

FAR → **THAT**

Those are my kites.

FAR → **THOSE**

LET'S PLAY

1 Complete the sentences with **these** or **those**.

a)

_____ are our backpacks.

b)

_____ are the balls we use in the gym class.

c)

_____ are healthy foods: fruits, milk, and salad.

d)

_____ are business buildings.

e)

_____ are my dolls.

f)

_____ are the Municipal Theater and the Botanical Garden.

2 Answer the questions with **this is** or **these are**.

a) What is this?

b) What are these?

3 Look at the picture and answer the question: Which demonstrative pronoun Emily has to use to talk about...

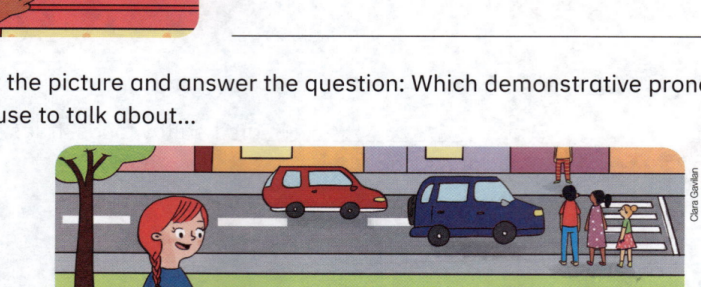

a) the people?

b) the dog and the cat?

c) her blue T-shirt?

d) the red car?

Friendships are essential in our lives!

Friendship provides us with good companionship and care.

A friend is someone we can trust and someone who helps us at any time. It is important to treat our friends nicely and with respect.

List in the chart below tips for being a great classmate.

A great classmate is	A great classmate

A great classmate says	A great classmate is not

ENGLISH AROUND THE WORLD

Summer camp

Summer camps are very popular in English-speaking countries. They are a great opportunity to make new friends and learn new things. Let's research what children do at summer camps in the United States, Canada, and England. Then color the pictures.

LET'S SING!

Make new friends

Make new friends,
but *keep* the old.
One is silver,
the other is gold.

A circle is round,
it has no end.
That's *how long*
I will be your friend.

A fire *burns* bright,
it *warms* the heart.
We've been friends
from the very start.

You have one hand,
I have the other.
Put them together,
we have each other.

Silver is precious,
gold is too.
I am precious
and so are you.

Across the land,
across the sea.
Friends forever
we will always be.

Traditional scout song. Adapted.

VOCABULARY

Across: através (de).
Burns (to burn): queima (queimar).
How long: por quanto tempo.
Keep (to keep): mantenha (manter).
Put (to put): coloque (colocar).
Warms (to warm): aquece (aquecer).

LITERARY TIME

Let's read a Garfield's comic strip!

The cat Garfield and the dog Oddie are good friends, but they love teasing each other!

1 What scares Garfield?

- The sounds Oddie makes.
- The coffee Garfield drinks.

2 What sounds does Oddie make?

- Yip.
- Bark.
- Yeah.

3 How does Garfield feel about Oddie?

- He is happy.
- He is annoyed.

LET'S LISTEN

1 Listen to the dialogue and fill in the blanks. Then circle Julia's pencil case.

Teacher Adam: Come on, kids, break time!

Liz: Come on, _____! Let's go!

Julia: I don't know where _____ is!

Liz: Is it one of _____ over there?

Julia: No. _____ ones are Tim's and Jonas' pencil cases. Mine is a pink one.

Liz: Oh, let's see! _____ is mine, and _____ one is Pamela's. Look. There is one pencil case under _____ chair!

Julia: Yes! _____ is my pencil case!

2 What are Julia and Liz looking for?

⬜ Liz's pencil case.

⬜ Pamela's pencil case.

⬜ Julia's pencil case.

DIGITAL PLAY

Inviting a friend via cell phone

Paste the stickers to complete the messages.

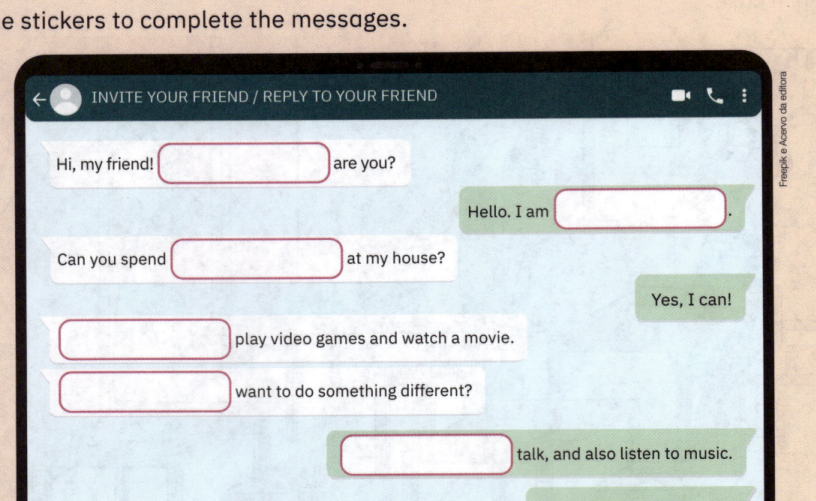

AFTER THIS UNIT I CAN

Greet people, invite a friend in, reply to a friend.

Identify demonstrative pronouns.

Identify and use the Simple Present.

Recognize the importance of friendship and how to be a good colleague.

Understand that summer camps offer us an opportunity to make friends and learn to live together.

UNIT 4 AT THE CAFETERIA

VOCABULARY

Chicken: frango.	**Pasta:** macarrão.
Hot dog: cachorro-quente.	**Soda:** refrigerante.
Juice: suco.	**Steak:** bife.
Order: pedido.	**Vegetable salad:** salada de legumes.

COMPREHENSION

1 Where are the students?

☐ At the cafeteria.

☐ At the food court.

2 Match the food item with the student who ordered it. Then write the price of their meal.

a)

Julia

Hot dog and orange juice.

_____

b)

Jeremy

Vegetable salad and steak.

_____

c)

Jonas

Hamburger and soda.

_____

d)

Liz

Pasta and chicken.

_____

3 Circle the healthy food and cross out the junk food.

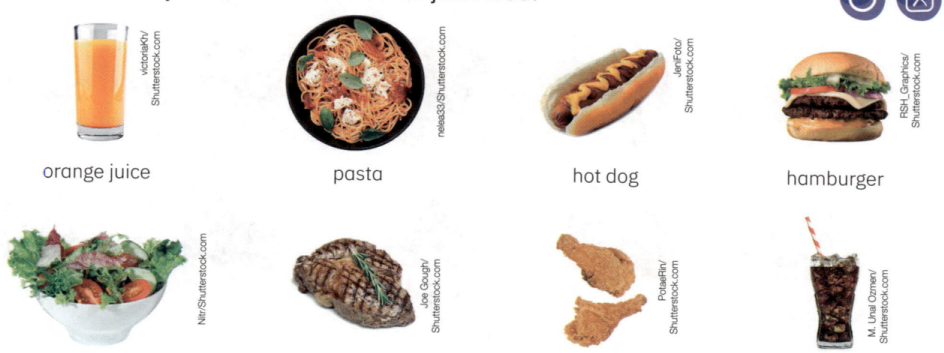

orange juice · pasta · hot dog · hamburger · salad · steak · fried chicken · soda

4 Who ordered healthy food?

☐ _iz and Jonas. ☐ Julia and Jeremy.

LET'S PLAY

1 What would they like to eat? Observe the images and answer.

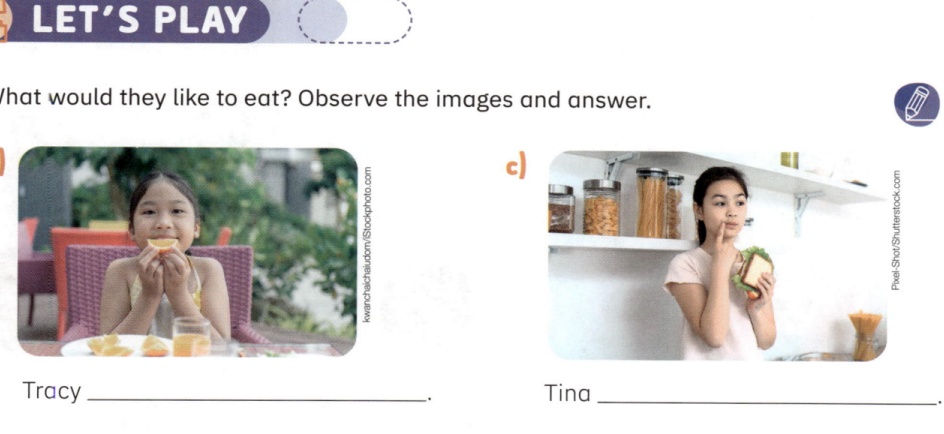

a) Tracy _____.

b) Pamela _____.

c) Tina _____.

d) Carol _____ cone.

2 What would you like to eat? Choose the food items you like and create a meal.

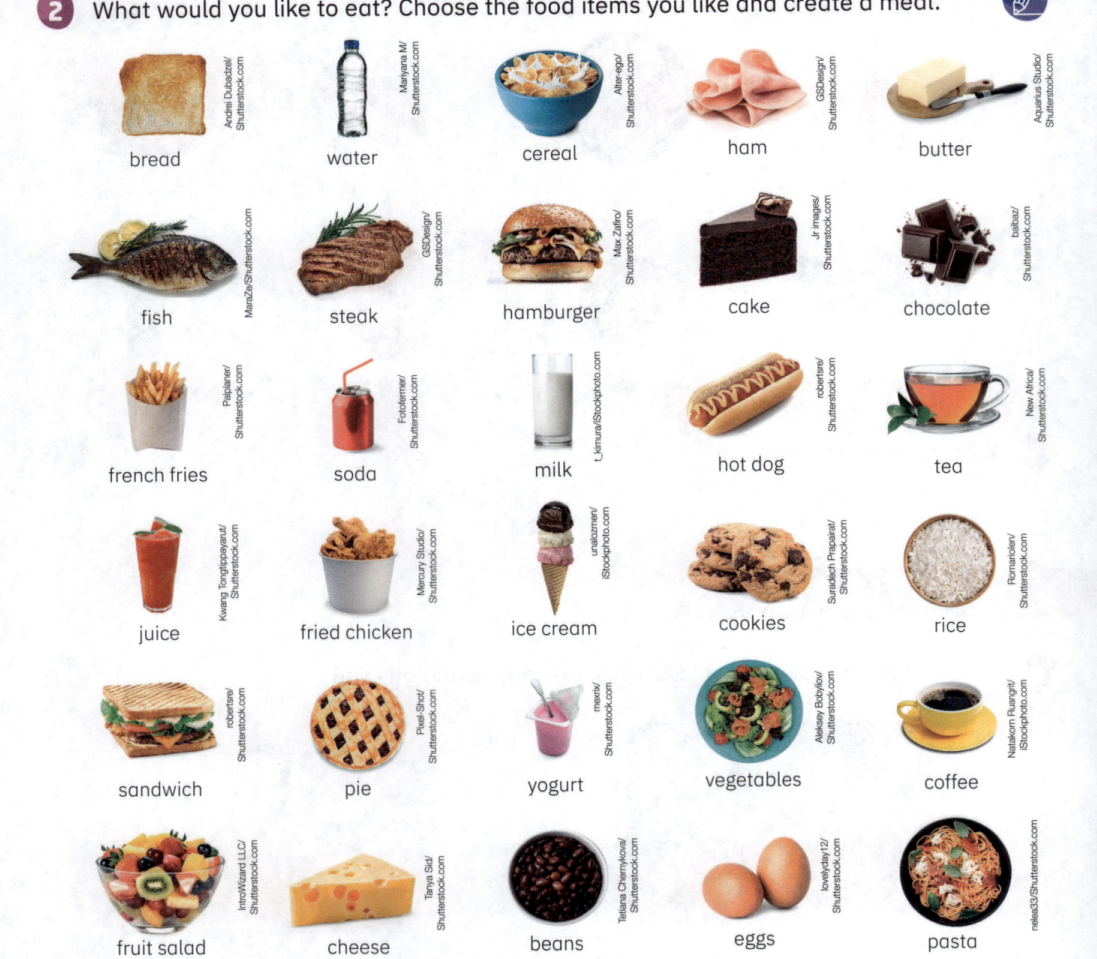

Beverages	**Main dish**	**Desserts**

GRAMMAR POINT

Modal – would like

It is used to make polite requests.

It is used as a synonym of **want**.

Observe:

LET'S PLAY

1 Find ten differences in the pictures below.

Five crispy pancakes

Five crispy pancakes in a **frying pan**,
flip them and **catch** them if you can.
Along came Rachel for a pancake one day.
Mom **sprinkled** it with sugar, and she **took it away**.

Four **crispy** pancakes in a frying pan,
flip them and catch them if you can.
Along came Ethan for a pancake one day.
Mom sprinkled it with **sugar**, and he took it away.

Three crispy pancakes in a frying pan,
flip them and catch them if you can.
Along came Barry for a pancake one day.
Mom sprinkled it with sugar, and he took it away.

Two crispy pancakes in a frying pan,
flip them and catch them if you can.
Along came Kate for a pancake one day.
Mom sprinkled it with sugar, and she took it away.

One crispy pancake in a frying pan,
flip it and catch it if you can.
Along came David for a pancake one day.
Mom sprinkled it with sugar, and he took it away.
No more pancakes in the frying pan!

Nursery rhyme. Adapted.

LET'S SING!

 VOCABULARY

Catch (to catch): pegue (pegar).
Crispy: crocante.
Flip (to flip): vire (virar).
Frying pan: frigideira.

Sprinkled (to sprinkle): polvilhou (polvilhar).
Sugar: açúcar.
Took it away (to take away): levou embora (levar embora).

DIGITAL PLAY

Children's healthy plate at school

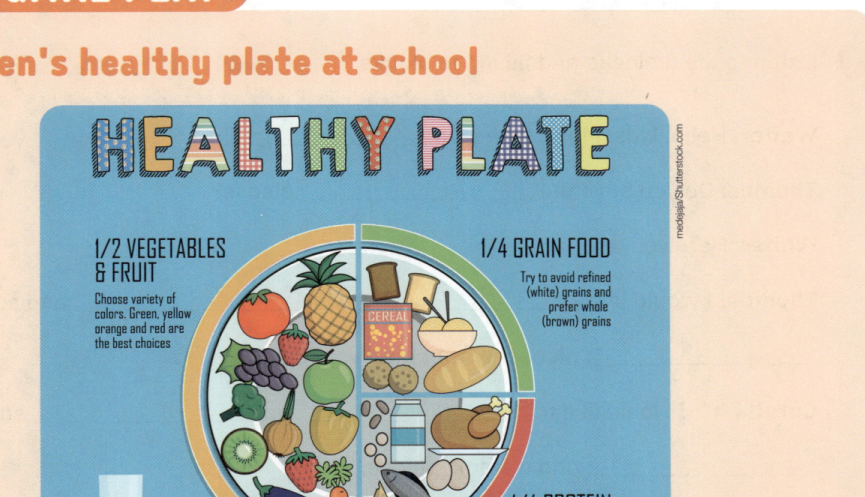

Write four food items you see on the plate.

ENGLISH AROUND THE WORLD

Discover the typical breakfast in some countries

Unscramble the letters, find words, and name the pictures.

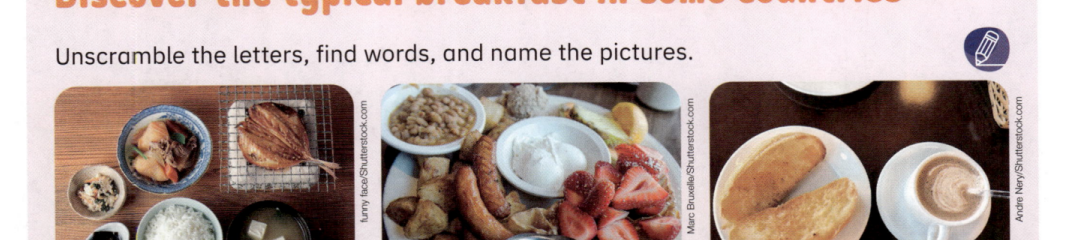

tsafkareb seenapaJ · tsafkareb naidanCa · tsafkareb zinaliBra

1 Listen to the dialogue and fill in the blanks.

Waiter: Hello, kids. May I take your _____?

Thomas: Do you have the _____, please?

Waiter: Here you are.

Thomas: I would like _____ with _____ and some _____, please! What about you, Carol?

Carol: Oh... I would like a _____ and _____ salad, _____, and a steak, please.

Waiter: OK! I will be back in a minute with your orders!

2 Now draw what Carol ordered in the restaurant.

LITERARY TIME

Let's read a Monica's Gang comic strip!

Jimmy Five and Maggie went to the snack bar together.

1 What are Maggie and Jimmy Five drinking?

- Some soda.
- A milkshake.
- Some juice.

2 What is the polite way to ask for a snack?

- I want a milkshake.
- I would like a milkshake, please.

1 Listen and paste the stickers for the indicated food items in the appropriate box.

Healthy food

Junk food

1 Match the food items with their food groups.

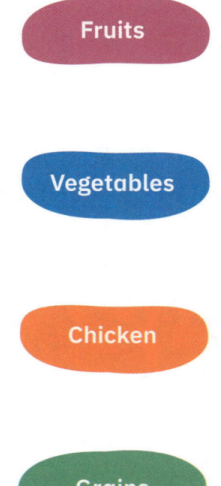

2 Now create a menu for a balanced meal you would like to eat. Then draw this meal.

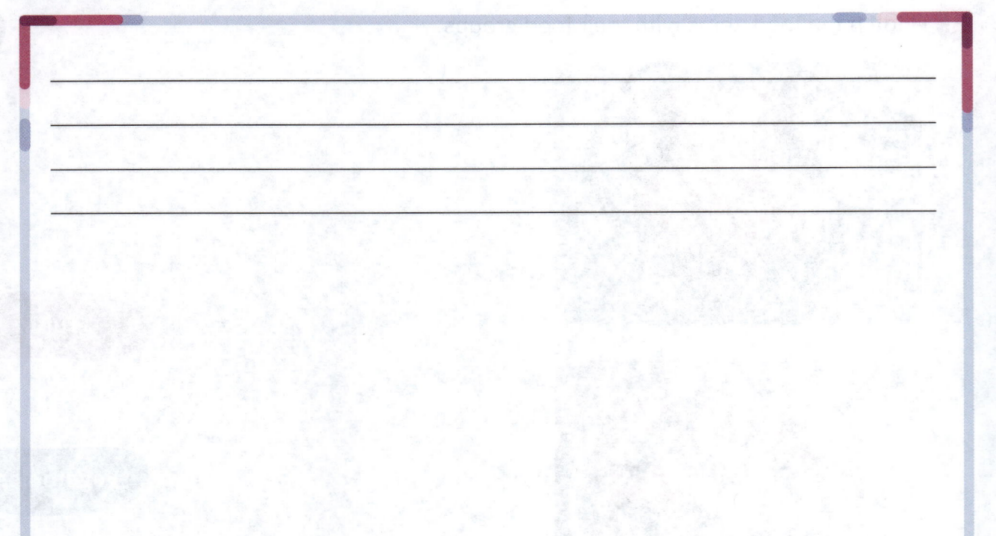

AFTER THIS UNIT I CAN

Identify different kinds of food.			
Identify and use the verb to be.			
Use the expression *I would like*.			
Learn about healthy food, junk food, and typical food.			

UNIT 5 THE FUN VISIT TO THE MUSEUM

 VOCABULARY

American Museum of Natural History: Museu Americano de História Natural.
Know (to know): sabem (saber).
Most: mais.
Museum: museu.

Place: lugar.
Scientific and cultural institution: instituição científica e cultural.
Several: diversos, vários.
World: mundo.

COMPREHENSION

1 **Choose the correct option.**

a) Where are the students going the next day?

☐ To the movie theater. ☐ To the museum.

b) What is there at the museum?

☐ Famous people. ☐ Fossils of dinosaurs. ☐ Famous inventions.

c) Why are they going there?

☐ Because it is old. ☐ Because it is interesting and important.

2 **Paste the stickers. Mark with an X what the children are going to see at the museum.**

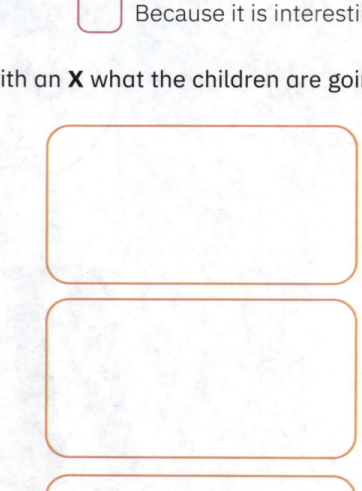

☐ Dinosaurs

☐ Paintings

☐ Mammoths

Interrogative pronouns (Question words)

They are used to ask a question.

WHAT ⟶ o que ou qual
What are the students going to do?
They are going to a field trip.

WHO ⟶ quem
Who is going to the field trip?
The teacher and the students.

WHEN ⟶ quando
When are the students going to the museum?
They are going there on June 22nd.

WHERE ⟶ onde ou aonde
Where are the students going?
They are going to the American Museum of Natural History.

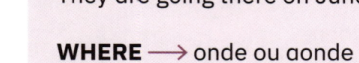

 Match the question words with their answers.

a) What — To the American Museum of Natural History.

b) When — A field trip.

c) Where — Because it is interesting and important.

d) Why — Tomorrow.

e) Who — Teacher and students.

Complete the questions with **what** or **who**.

a) _____ is there in your backpack?

b) _____ is the person with Julia?

 Where or when? Choose the best option.

a) Panama.

☐ When ☐ Where

b) Nine o'clock.

☐ When ☐ Where

c) New York.

☐ When ☐ Where

d) Next Friday.

☐ When ☐ Where

 Complete the sentences using **where** or **when**.

a) _____ is the museum?

b) _____ is our visit to the museum?

c) _____ does he arrive at school?

d) _____ do you live?

 Complete the sentences using **where**, **when**, **what** or **who**. Then answer about yourself.

a) _____ time do you go to school?

_____

b) _____ is your best friend?

_____

c) _____ is the school?

_____

d) _____ is your birthday?

_____

GOOD DEED

Museum at school

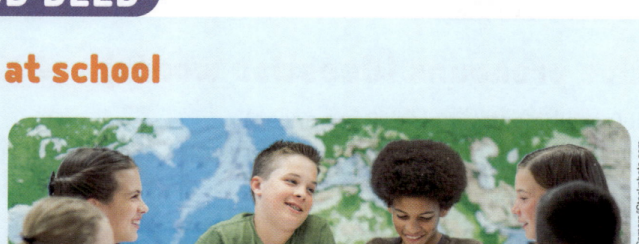

1 **Read and answer the questions orally.**

a) Do you know how important your school is?

b) How old is your school?

c) What is the history of your school?

2 **Draw the school entrance or your favorite school space. Write its name.**

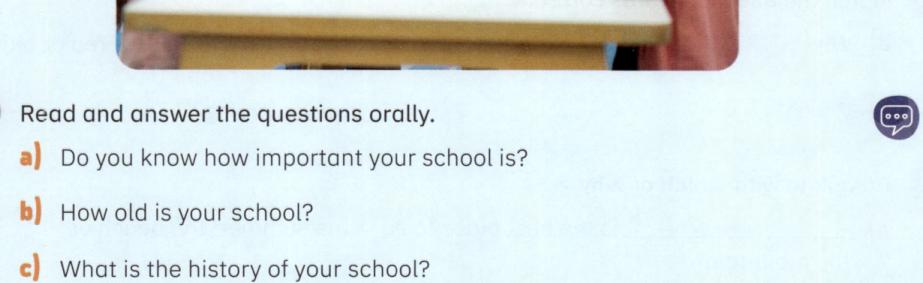

A_B^C GRAMMAR POINT

Interrogative pronouns (Question words)

WHICH —> qual (escolha entre mais de uma opção)
Which museum are they visiting — the Natural History or the Art Museum?

WHY —> por que (pergunta)
Why are they going to the museum?

LET'S PLAY

1 Match the question words correctly.

a) Why — is your favorite color — red or blue?

b) Which — are you crying?

2 Complete with **which** or **why**.

a) _____ is the best place to go in the summer: the beach or the mountain?

b) _____ is there a book here?

c) _____ are you going to the theater today?

d) _____ kind of fruit do you like: sweet or citric?

3 Which fruit do you like? Look and circle. Write the names of four of them.

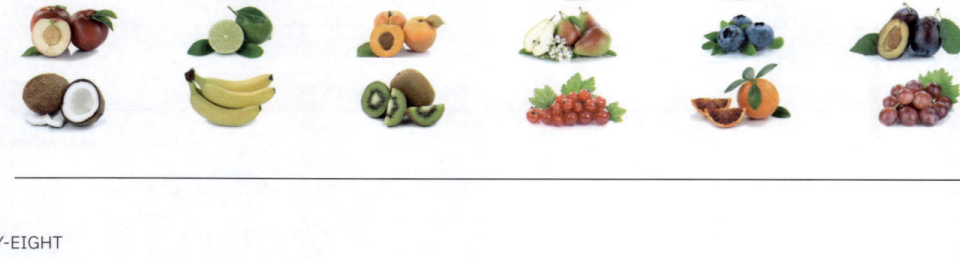

DIGITAL PLAY

Discover the Louvre Museum and the famous Mona Lisa

Write the name of the museum where the Mona Lisa painting is located.

___

ENGLISH AROUND THE WORLD

The Museums of English-speaking countries

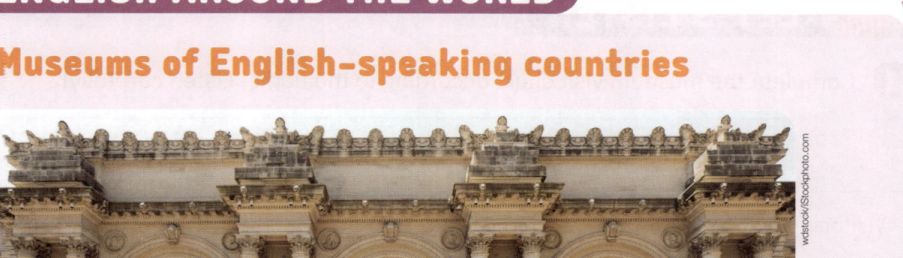

Write the name and acronym of the Museum of New York, the USA.

___

1 Write the numbers in full. Follow the example.

a) 49 – forty-nine

b) 43 – _____

c) 56 – _____

d) 62 – _____

e) 99 – _____

f) 71 – _____

2 Write the numbers in numerical form.

a) ten – _____

b) twenty – _____

c) thirty – _____

d) forty – _____

e) forty-three – _____

f) fifty – _____

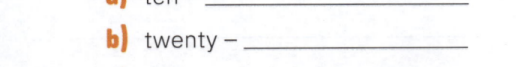

1 Complete the museum visit chart according to the audio. Listen carefully!

	Sunday	**Monday**	**Tuesday**	**Wednesday**	**Thursday**	**Friday**	**Saturday**
Visitors	**25**		**7**		**33**	**15**	

2 Listen, read, and complete the field trip authorization.

Class field trip

_____ are the students going?

They are going to the _____.

_____ is the class field trip?

It is on _____.

_____ is going to the field trip?

_____ are going to the field trip.

Calendar song

LET'S SING!

Twenty-four hours **make** a day,
time **enough** for work and play.

Seven days a week will make,
you will **learn** if lessons you **take**.

Fifty-two weeks make a year,
soon a new one will be here.

Twelve long months a year will make,
say them now without **mistake**.

Thirty days have September,
April, June, and November,
all the rest have thirty-one.

February **stands** alone,
twenty-eight days is all his share.
With 29 in each **leap year**,
that you may the leap year know.

Divide by 4 and that will show,
in each year are seasons 4,
you will learn I am sure:
Spring and summer, then fall,
winter last, but best of all.

Public domain song. Adapted.

 VOCABULARY

Enough: suficiente.
Leap year: ano bissexto.
Learn (to learn): aprender.
Make (to make): faz (fazer).

Mistake: erro.
Soon: em breve.
Stands (to stand): permanece (permanecer).
Take (to take): tomar.

LET'S PLAY

1 Have you ever been to these famous museums?

a) Imperial Museum, Petrópolis.

☐ Yes.

☐ No.

b) MASP, São Paulo.

☐ Yes.

☐ No.

c) Oscar Niemeyer Museum, Curitiba.

☐ Yes.

☐ No.

2 How should we behave when we visit a museum? Check the correct actions.

☐ We should touch the objects.

☐ We should walk, not run.

☐ We should respect others.

☐ We should eat and drink during the visit.

☐ We should pay attention and ask questions.

☐ We should enjoy the visit and have fun!

Complete the pyramid writing the numbers sequence.

AFTER THIS UNIT I CAN

	😊	😐	😟
Greet people and talk to them.			
Reply to people.			
Identify the numbers from 10 to 100.			
Use interrogative pronouns.			
Talk about art and culture.			
Understand the importance of museums.			
Talk about how to behave in museums.			

COMPREHENSION

1 Where are the kids?

☐ In a gym class.

☐ In a music class.

☐ In a math class.

2 Match the kid and his/her favorite music style.

a)  Carol

• classical

b)  Thomas

• jazz

c)  Tim

• rock

d)  Pamela

• *samba*

GRAMMAR POINT

Verb TO BE

The verb **to be** (**am**, **is**, or **are**) is used to talk about feelings, location, identity, and quality.

Feelings

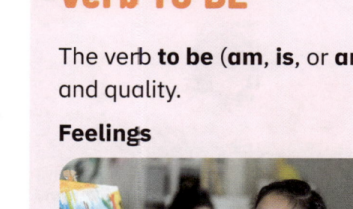

I **am** happy.

Identity

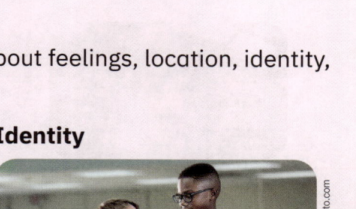

They **are** Jonas and Tim.

Location

Roberta **is** next to Jonas.

Quality

The flowers **are** beautiful.

Now look how the verb is conjugated:

Subject pronoun	Verb to be
I	am
You	are
He	is
She	is
It	is
We	are
You	are
They	are

1 Are they happy with the soundtrack? Circle how they feel about it.

a)

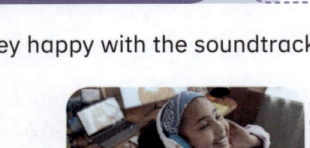

👍 Yes, I am happy. 👎 No, I am not happy.

b)

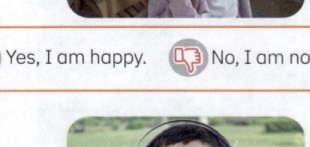

👍 Yes, I am happy. 👎 No, I am not happy.

c)

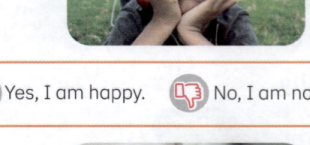

👍 Yes, I am happy. 👎 No, I am not happy.

d)

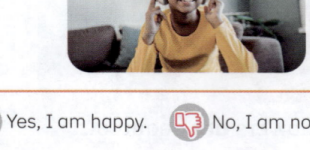

👍 Yes, I am happy. 👎 No, I am not happy.

e)

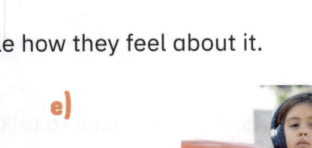

👍 Yes, I am happy. 👎 No, I am not happy.

f)

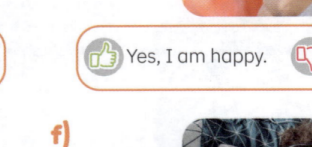

👍 Yes, I am happy. 👎 No, I am not happy.

g)

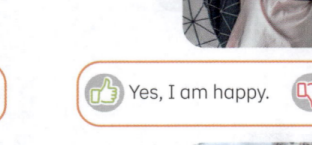

👍 Yes, I am happy. 👎 No, I am not happy.

h)

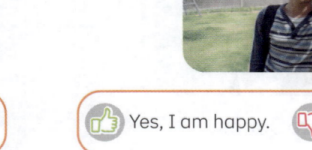

👍 Yes, I am happy. 👎 No, I am not happy.

2 Read and complete the sentences with the verb **to be**.

a) John _____ tall.

b) Suzy _____ from Rio.

c) I _____ a student.

d) They _____ boys.

3 **Choose the best option. Then complete the sentences.**

a) Liz _____ a good student.

☐ am
☐ is
☐ are

b) I _____ sick.

☐ am
☐ is
☐ are

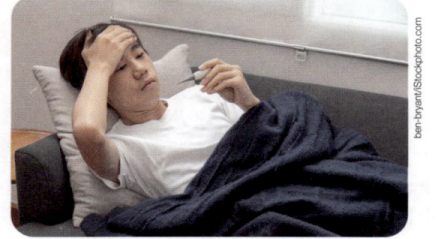

c) They _____ Thomas' parents.

☐ am
☐ is
☐ are

d) The rock concert _____ in the park.

☐ am
☐ is
☐ are

Music man

LET'S SING!

I am the music man, I come from *far away*
and I **can play**.
What can you play?
I play the piano,
pia-pia-pia-no, piano, piano,
pia-pia-pia-no, pia-piano!

I am the music man, I come from far away
and I can play.
What can you play?
I play the **bells**,
jing a ling a ling a ling, jing a ling, jing a ling,
jing a ling a ling a ling, jing a ling a ling!

I am the music man, I come from far away
and I can play.
What can you play?
I play the **tambourine**,
chink a chink a chink a chink, chink a chink, chink a chink,
chink a chink a chink a chink, chink a chink a chink!

I am the music man, I come from far away
and I can play.
What can you play?
I play the **wood blocks**,
tap a tap a tap a tap, tap a tap, tap a tap,
tap a tap a tap a tap, tap a tap a tap!

I am the music man, I come from far away
and I can play.
What can you play?
I play the **shakers**,
shaky shaky shaky shake, shaky shake, shaky shake,
shaky shaky shaky shake, shaky shaky shake!

Cumulative folk song. Adapted.

VOCABULARY

Bell(s): sino(s).
Can: pode (poder, conseguir).
Far away: longe.
Play (to play): tocar.

Shaker(s): chocalho(s).
Tambourine: pandeiro.
Wood block(s): bloco(s) de madeira.

LET'S PLAY

1 What kind of music are they playing? Choose the correct music style from the box.

rock * jazz * samba * pop * classical * country

LET'S LISTEN

Learn the names of some musical instruments.

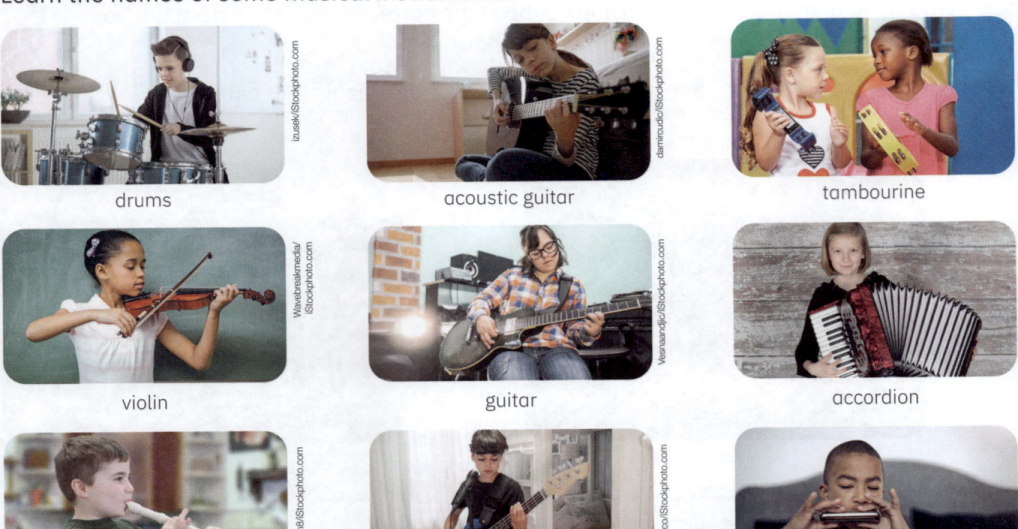

1 Listen and write the musical instruments mentioned in each music genre.

a) Classical music: _____.

b) Jazz: _____.

c) Country: _____.

d) Rock: _____.

e) *Samba*: _____.

f) Pop: _____.

LITERARY TIME

The pied piper of Hamelin

The city of Hamelin had a big problem: it was full of rats. One day, a **stranger**, with a flute, came to the town and told the **mayor**:

"I can **get rid of** all the rats. What would my **reward** be?"

The mayor answered:

"Ten thousand gold coins from our treasure!"

The stranger walked out into the street and started to play his flute.

A mysterious sound **floated** in the air, and all the people of Hamelin could hear the beautiful tune.

All of a sudden, thousands of rats came all the way from various directions and **followed** that mysterious sound from the piper's flute.

The stranger **kept** playing the flute and walked right into the sea. The rats followed him there, and all of them were **caught** by the **waves**.

German legend. Pied Piper of Hamelin. Adapted.

VOCABULARY

All of a sudden: de repente.
Caught (to catch): pegos (pegar).
Floated (to float): flutuou (flutuar).
Followed (to follow): seguiu (seguir).
Get rid of (to get rid of): livrar-se de.
Kept (to keep): continuou (continuar, manter).

Mayor: prefeito(a).
Piper: flautista.
Reward: recompensa, prêmio.
Stranger: forasteiro, pessoa desconhecida.
Wave(s): onda(s).

1 What instrument did the piper play? Circle it.

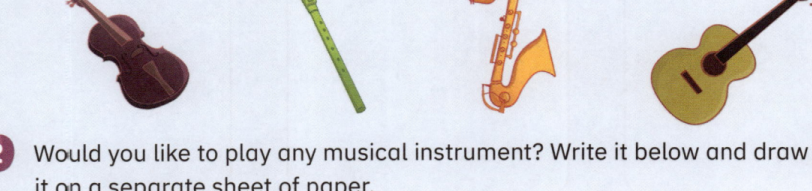

2 Would you like to play any musical instrument? Write it below and draw it on a separate sheet of paper.

 Listen and apply stickers to each character according to their favorite musical style.

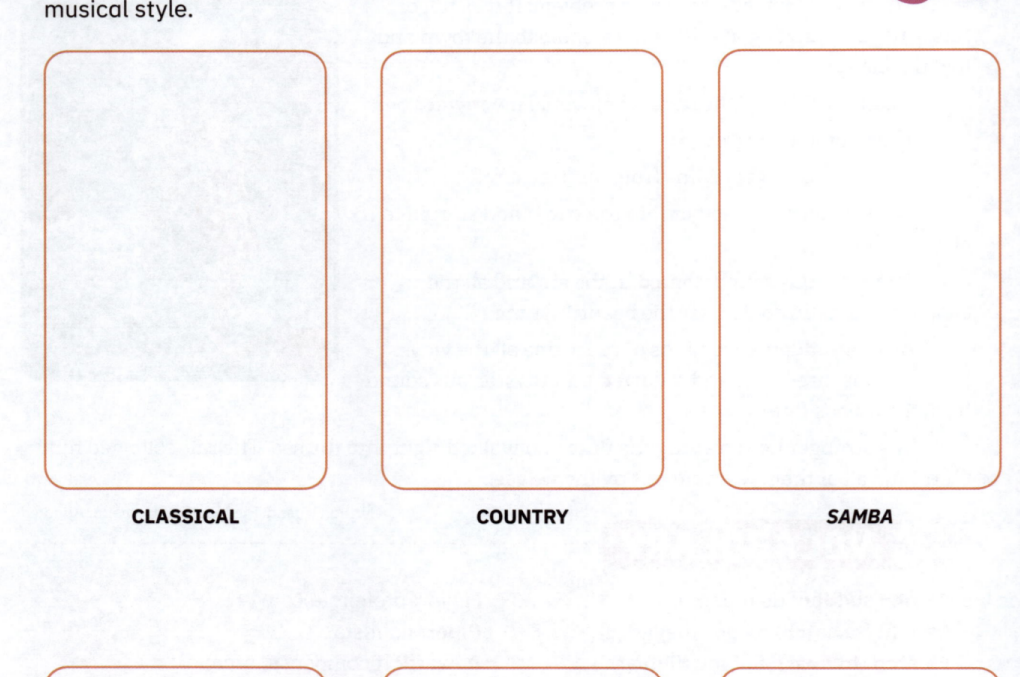

CLASSICAL | **COUNTRY** | ***SAMBA***

ROCK | **JAZZ** | **POP**

 Draw a picture of yourself. Then complete your file.

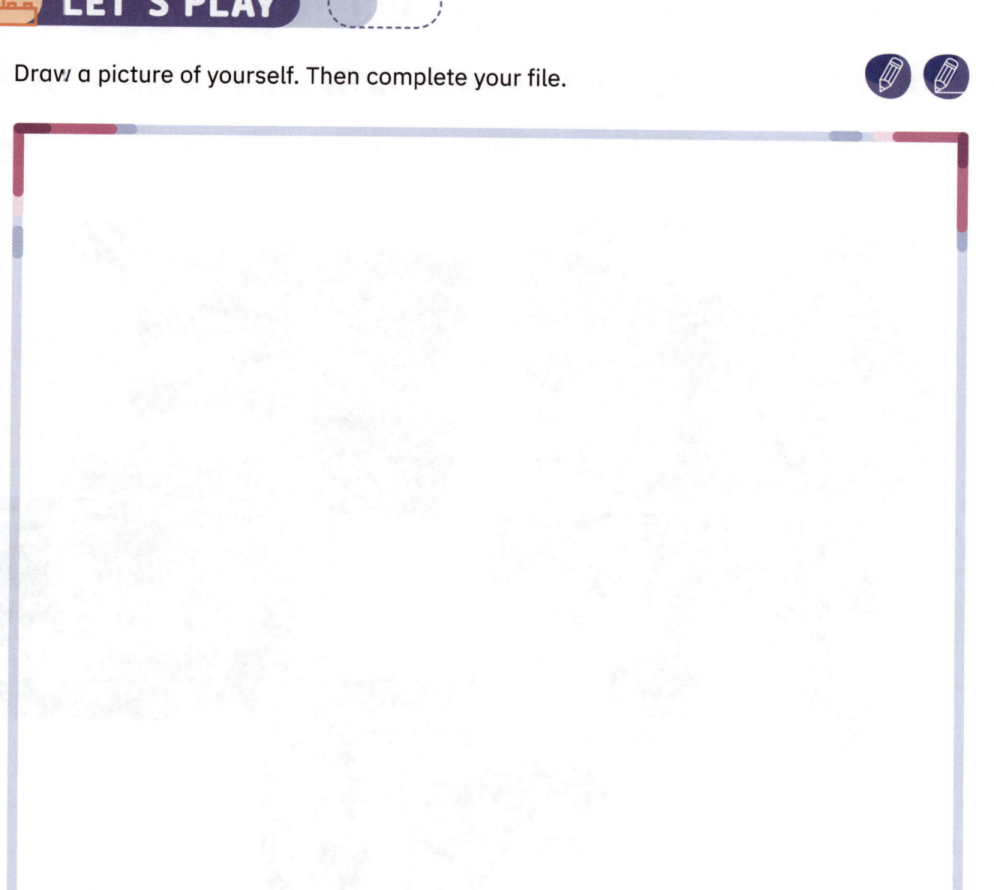

My favorite musical style is:

My favorite musical instrument is:

ENGLISH AROUND THE WORLD

The African Cultural influence in Brazil and the USA

Do you know the influence of African culture on music in Brazil and the United States? Let's research!

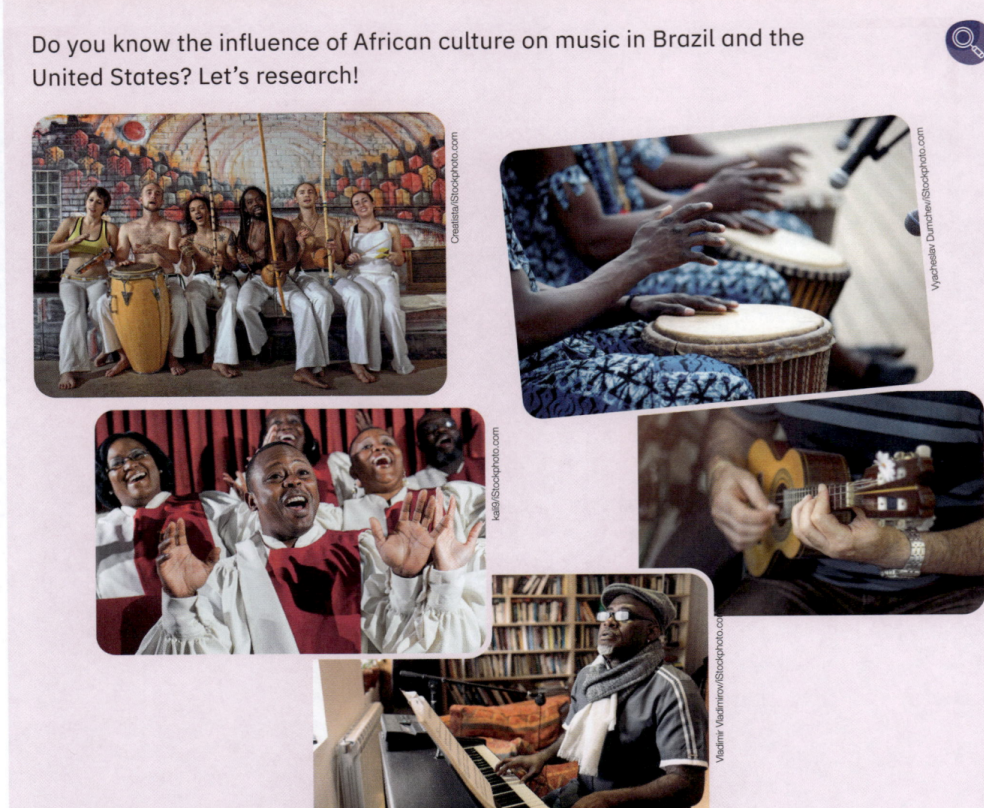

What rhythms or musical styles did you find in your research?

In Brazil

_____

_____

In the United States

_____

_____

DIGITAL PLAY

Do you know the differences among the different kinds of instruments?

1 Research and answer: What are wind, string, and percussion instruments?

_____

_____

_____

2 Choose one instrument and research how it is made.

_____

_____

3 Make your musical instrument! Draw it.

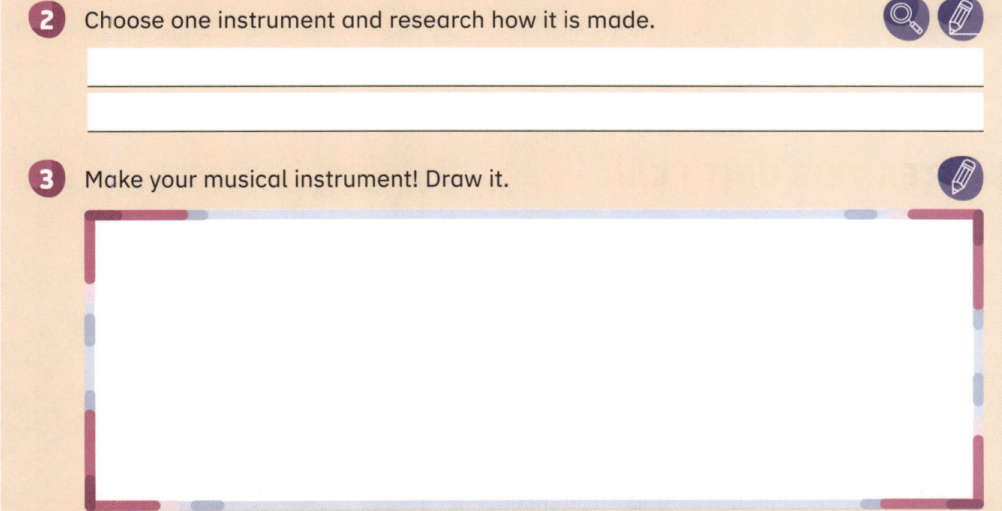

1 Look at the pictures and complete the sentences using the verb **to be**.

a)

They _____ musicians in an orchestra.

b)

He _____ a bass player in a rock band.

c)

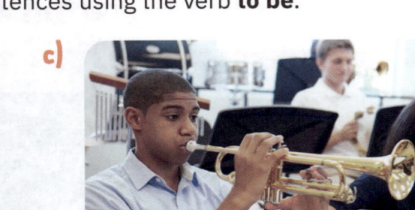

He _____ playing the trumpet.

It _____ a wind instrument.

d)

They _____ playing *samba*.

AFTER THIS UNIT I CAN

Greet people, ask them questions, and reply to theirs.

Identify adjectives.

Identify and use the Simple Present tense of verbs.

Identify and classify musical instruments.

Recognize musical genres.

Understand the influence of African culture on the Brazilian and North American music.

 COMPREHENSION

1 Where are Julia and her mother going?

☐ To the drugstore.

☐ To the food court.

☐ To the shopping mall.

2 Where do they go to look for these items? Match.

a) sneakers • outlet store

b) skirt • bookstore

c) book • shoe store

3 Which clothing items is Julia looking for? Circle and color them.

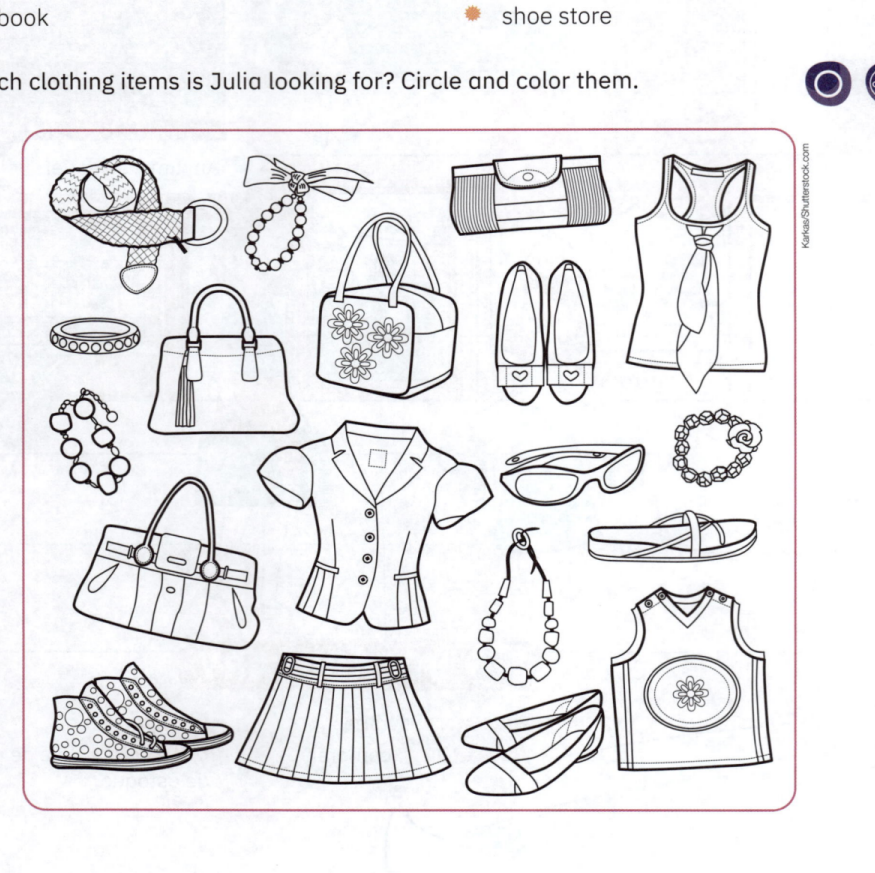

LET'S PLAY

1 Look at the pictures and write what the characters need to buy.

a) _____

b) _____

c) _____

d) _____

2 What can you find in each place? Write it down.

Foods and drinks * Books * Clothes and shoes * Movies and plays

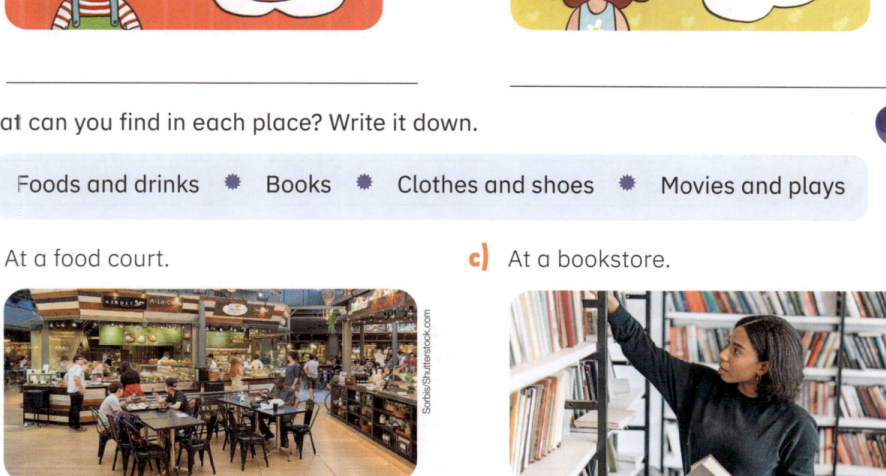

a) At a food court.

_____

b) At a department store.

_____

c) At a bookstore.

_____

d) At the movies or at the theater.

_____

3 Choose the correct word according to the piece of clothing.

a) hot · hat · het · hut
○ · ○ · ○ · ○

b) shirts · shotrs · sherts · shorts
○ · ○ · ○ · ○

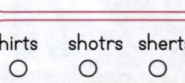

c) bolt · balt · delt · belt
○ · ○ · ○ · ○

d) t-shirt · t-shitr · t-shert · t-short
○ · ○ · ○ · ○

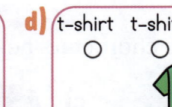

e) jocket · jekcet · jacket · jasket
○ · ○ · ○ · ○

f) truser · thousers · troser · trousers
○ · ○ · ○ · ○

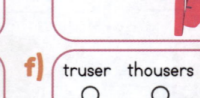

g) socks · sacks · sucks · soksc
○ · ○ · ○ · ○

h) sheos · shues · shoes · shaes
○ · ○ · ○ · ○

i) hodei · hoodie · heidie · haadie
○ · ○ · ○ · ○

4 Unscramble the letters.

a) SROEBOKOT _____

b) SERDS _____

c) PLFI-LOFPS _____

d) SVMOIE _____

e) NPTSA _____

f) TRISH _____

g) HOSES _____

h) SDASNAL _____

5 Read and guess the place.

a) People go there to buy skirts, shirts and other items of clothing.

_____

b) People go there to eat and drink.

_____

c) People go there to shop for several things.

_____

LET'S PLAY

1 Let's play bingo!

dress * flip-flops * jeans * pants * sandals * shoes * shorts
skirt * sneakers * socks * T-shirt * underwear * movies
food court * shirt * department store * bookstore * theater

DIGITAL PLAY

Discover RESO, Montreal's underground city

Write down the length (in kilometers) of the RESO complex in Montreal, Canada.

ENGLISH AROUND THE WORLD

Curiosities about RESO, Montreal's underground city

Write three places that the underground city of RESO, in Montreal, Canada, connects you to.

LET'S SING!

One, two, let's buy my shoe

One, two,
let's buy my **shoe**.

Three, four,
let's go to the **store**.

Five, six,
make a clothing mix.

Seven, eight,
it's a buying **trade**.

Nine, ten,
let's shop **again**.

Eleven, twelve,
things on the **shelves**.

Thirteen, fourteen,
the **clothes** are **clean**.

Fifteen, sixteen,
wear your jeans.

Seventeen, eighteen,
never wear green.

Nineteen, twenty,
I **spent** my last **penny**!

Nursery rhyme. Adapted.

VOCABULARY

Again: novamente.
Clean: limpas.
Clothes: roupas.
Penny: centavo.
Shelves: prateleiras.

Shoe: sapato.
Spent (to spend): gastei (gastar).
Store: loja.
Trade: comércio.
Wear (to wear): vista (vestir).

1 What are the boys looking for? Listen to the dialogue and color the items they need.

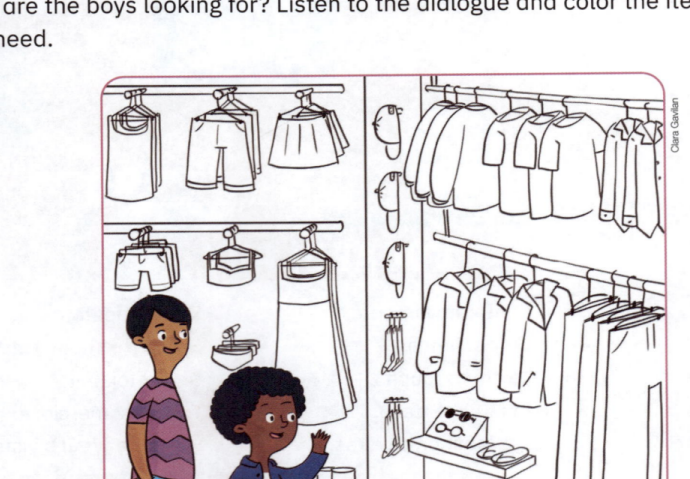

2 Listen to the dialogue again and answer the questions.

a) Where are Thomas and Tim?

☐ At a bookstore. ☐ At a food court. ☐ At the shopping mall.

b) Who is buying these items? Match.

- Thomas
- Tim

LITERARY TIME

The emperor's new clothes

"Once upon a time there was an emperor whose only interest in life was to dress up in fashionable clothes. [...]

Once, two **thieves** decided to teach him a lesson.

They told the emperor that they were very fine tailors and could sew a lovely new suit for him. It would be so light and fine that it would **seem invisible**. [...] The emperor was very excited and ordered the new tailors to begin their **work**. [..]

Finally, the emperor's new dress was ready. He could see nothing but he too did not want to appear stupid. [...] The people could only see a **naked** emperor but no one admitted it for fear of being thought **stupid**. [...]

At last, a child cried out, "The emperor is naked!"

The emperor's new clothes. *Short stories*, [*s. l.*], [201-]. Available at: https://shortstoriesshort.com/story/the-emperors-new-clothes/. Access: Nov. 5 2023.

VOCABULARY

Dress up (to dress up): arrumar-se.	**Seem (to seem):** parecer.
Emperor: imperador.	**Stupid:** estúpido, bobo.
Fashionable: na moda.	**Suit:** traje.
Invisible: invisível.	**Tailor(s):** alfaiate(s).
Naked: nu, nua.	**Thieves:** ladrões.
Once upon a time: era uma vez.	**Work:** trabalho.

1 Who decided to teach the emperor a lesson?

⬜ Two thieves.

⬜ A child.

2 What would the emperor's clothes look like?

⬜ Heavy and ugly.

⬜ Light and almost invisible.

1 Paste the stickers and unscramble the letters.

a) BEINAE _____

b) SWAETER _____

c) KOSCS _____

d) TOBSO _____

AFTER THIS UNIT I CAN

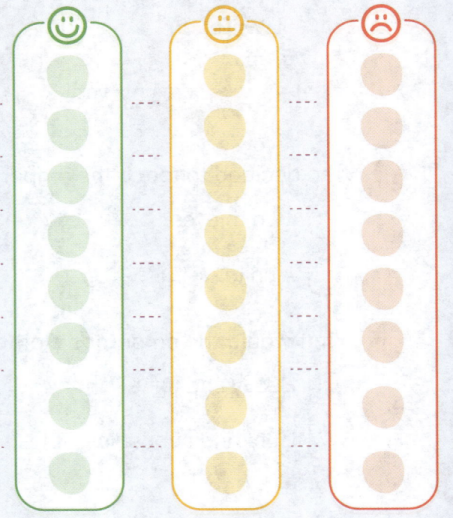

Identify the plural of nouns.

Reply to people's questions.

Identify words related to clothing.

Identify and use interrogative pronouns.

Identify different products.

Identify different places in a neighborhood.

Understand the importance of structures for living in countries with harsh winters.

Discover interesting facts about an underground city.

UNIT 8 DIFFERENT JOBS

VOCABULARY

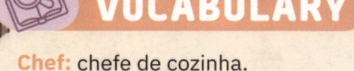

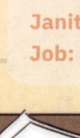

Chef: chefe de cozinha.
Doctor: médico(a).
Firefighter: bombeiro(a).
Janitor: zelador(a).
Job: profissão, emprego.

Judge: juiz, juíza.
Photographer: fotógrafo(a).
Pilot: piloto(a).
Professions: profissões.
Singer: cantor(a).

COMPREHENSION

1 What is the class about? Check the correct answer.

◯ The class is about different jobs. ◯ The class is about cities.

2 Write four professions mentioned in the class.

_____

_____

_____

_____

3 Let's learn some professions. Look at the pictures and write the missing words.

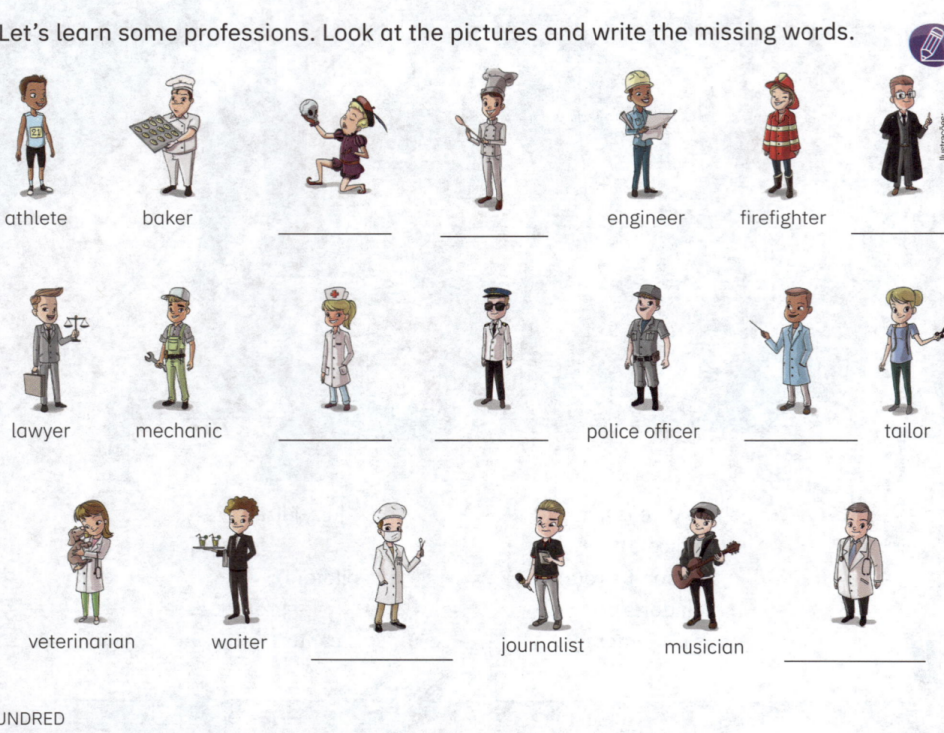

athlete | baker | _____ | _____ | engineer | firefighter | _____

lawyer | mechanic | _____ | _____ | police officer | _____ | tailor

veterinarian | waiter | _____ | journalist | musician | _____

1 What profession do these items refer to? Paste the stickers and complete the sentences.

a) Susan is a _____.

b) My mother and my father are _____.

c) My uncle is a _____.

d) Melissa is a _____.

2 Let's find ten jobs in the wordsearch.

baker • dentist
judge • mechanic
veterinarian • doctor
waiter • musician
janitor • police officer

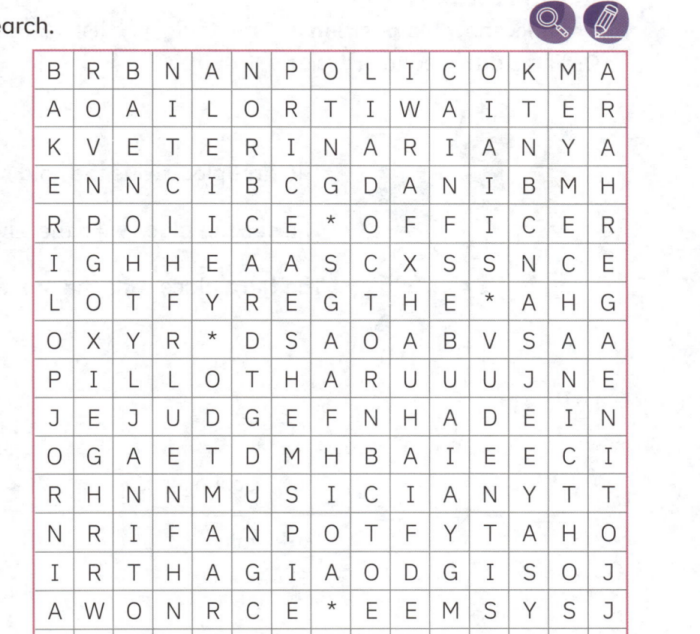

B	R	B	N	A	N	P	O	L	I	C	O	K	M	A
A	O	A	I	L	O	R	T	I	W	A	I	T	E	R
K	V	E	T	E	R	I	N	A	R	I	A	N	Y	A
E	N	N	C	I	B	C	G	D	A	N	I	B	M	H
R	P	O	L	I	C	E	*	O	F	F	I	C	E	R
I	G	H	H	E	A	A	S	C	X	S	S	N	C	E
L	O	T	F	Y	R	E	G	T	H	E	*	A	H	G
O	X	Y	R	*	D	S	A	O	A	B	V	S	A	A
P	I	L	L	O	T	H	A	R	U	U	U	J	N	E
J	E	J	U	D	G	E	F	N	H	A	D	E	I	N
O	G	A	E	T	D	M	H	B	A	I	E	E	C	I
R	H	N	N	M	U	S	I	C	I	A	N	Y	T	T
N	R	I	F	A	N	P	O	T	F	Y	T	A	H	O
I	R	T	H	A	G	I	A	O	D	G	I	S	O	J
A	W	O	N	R	C	E	*	E	E	M	S	Y	S	J
R	A	R	E	G	G	I	P	Y	A	N	T	T	S	A
G	S	A	E	S	T	Y	G	W	Y	E	F	I	E	T

Cardinal and ordinal numbers

Cardinal numbers

Cardinals show the **quantity** of something.
Cardinals are used to **count**.

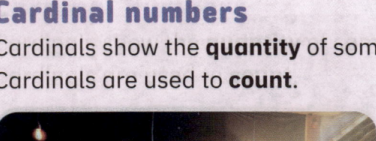

There are **five** musicians.

There are **six** doctors.

Ordinal numbers

Ordinals show the **position** of something on a list.
Ordinals are used to **ordenar**.

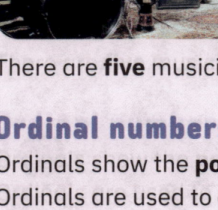

The **first** place wins the gold medal.

The **second** place wins the silver medal.

The **third** place wins the bronze medal.

Look:

1st = first	6th = sixth
2nd = second	7th = seventh
3rd = third	8th = eighth
4th = fourth	9th = ninth
5th = fifth	10th = tenth

LET'S PLAY

1 Look at the pictures and fill in the charts with the correct information.

1st: _____ picture	**2nd**: _____ picture
Job: _____	**Job**: _____
Quantity: _____	**Quantity**: _____

2 Complete with ordinal numbers.

a) 1st _____

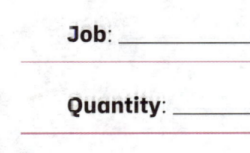

_____

b) 2nd _____

_____

c) 3rd _____

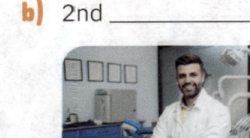

_____

d) 4th _____

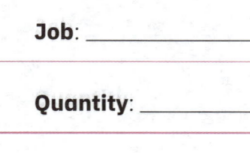

_____

e) 5th _____

_____

f) 6th _____

_____

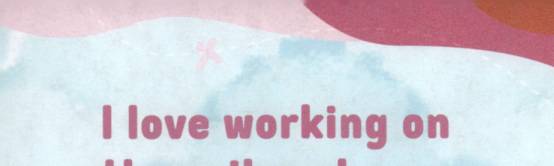

I love working on the railroad

LET'S SING!

I love working on the **railroad**
When I was **young** it was my dream... The train.

Chorus
Maybe a captain
Maybe a **chemist**
Maybe a dentist

Tickerty-tack... This is how we cross the road.
Always **pay close attention**.
Noisy little train!
To stop! Says Red Light.
And then the path continues.
Green cross code... Traffic lights.

Chorus
Maybe a captain
Maybe a chemist
Maybe a dentist

More and more women work on the **railway**
And so the world **evolves**
With good professionals

Chorus
Maybe a captain
Maybe a chemist
Maybe a dentist

Specially written for this book.

 VOCABULARY

Chemist: químico(a) (profissão).
Evolves (to evolve): evolui (evoluir).
Green cross code: código cruzado verde.
Pay close attention (to pay close attention): preste bastante atenção (prestar bastante atenção).

Railroad: ferrovia.
Railway: estrada de ferro.
Young: jovem.

ENGLISH AROUND THE WORLD

The exploration of child labor around the world

Write a warning sentence against the exploration of child labor.

_____

_____

DIGITAL PLAY

The digital culture and the new professions in the world

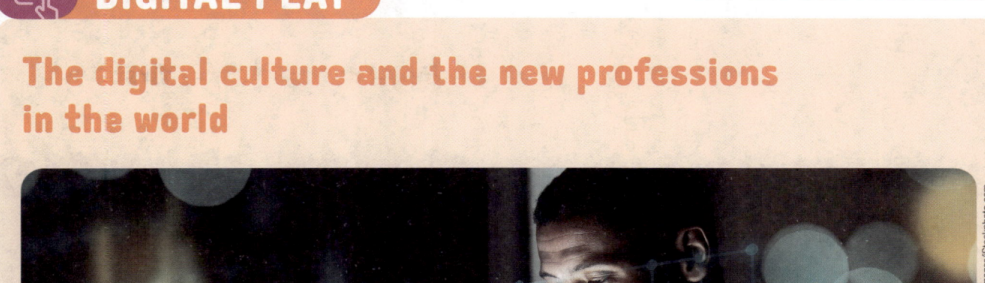

Read the sentences and write F (False) or T (True).

⬜ New professions around the world do not use technology.

⬜ The professions such as digital marketing, SEO analyst, social media specialist and web designer are new.

 Listen, circle the cardinal numbers, and cross out the ordinals.

24	**5**	**4th**	**ninety-six**
37	**3rd**	**nineteen**	**tenth**
48	**2nd**	**sixteen**	**sixth**
		thirty-one	**first**

 Listen to the dialogue and fill in the blanks.

Teacher Adam: What do you want to be when you grow up?

Henry: I want to be a _____ to put out _____.
And you, Alex?

Alex: I want to be a _____ and fly all around the _____.
Milena?

Milena: I want to be a _____ to help _____ people.
What about you, Thomas?

Thomas: I want to be a _____ to help children _____.
And you, Jeremy?

Jeremy: I want to be a _____; I love to bake _____ and cookies. Pamela, and you?

Pamela: I want to be an _____ to build lots of _____.
What about you, Jonas?

Jonas: I want to be a _____ and follow the _____.
Julia, and you?

Julia: I want to be a _____ and keep everybody _____!

LITERARY TIME

Charlie Brown and Linus

Read this dialogue.

 VOCABULARY

About: sobre.
All the time: o tempo todo.
Future: futuro.
Grow up (to grow up): crescer.

Much: muito.
Outrageously: escandalosamente.
Think (to think): pensa (pensar).
You'd like (you would like): você gostaria.

1 What is Charlie Brown talking about?

About the past.

About the future.

2 How does Linus want to be in the future?

Happy.

Sad.

3 Continue the story. Draw Linus in the future.

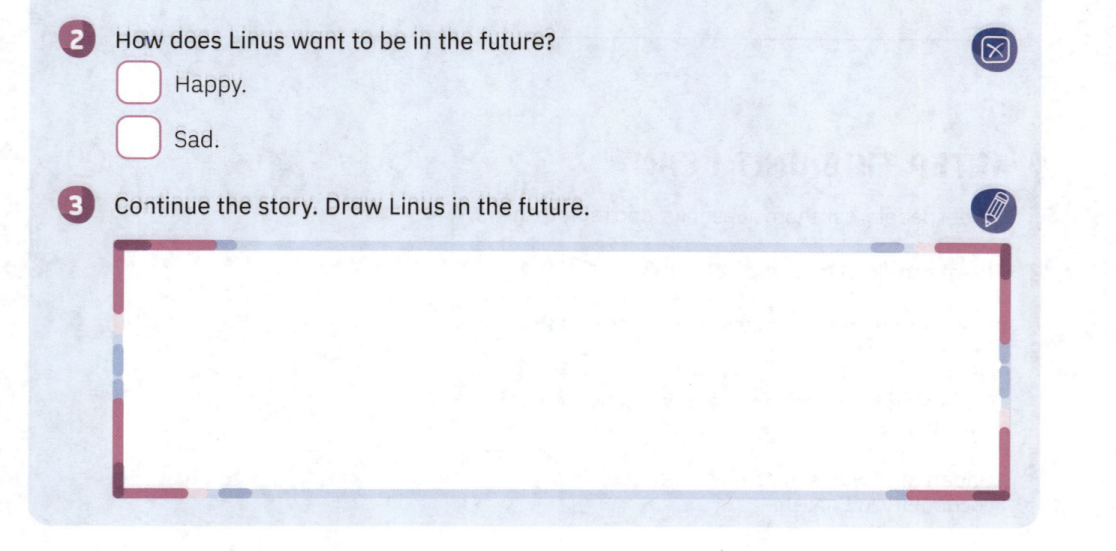

GOOD DEED

When I grow up...

Imagine what profession you would like to have when you grow up, then respond as your future self.

Profession: _____

1 How old are you? _____

2 What is your job? _____

3 What is your routine like? _____

_____

_____

4 Are you a good worker? _____

_____

_____

5 Are you happy in your profession? Why? _____

_____

_____

AFTER THIS UNIT I CAN

Greet people, ask them questions, and reply to theirs.

Identify ordinal and cardinal numbers.

Understand and use imagination to project the future.

Understand information about the exploration of child labor.

Understand words in context by developing vocabulary in English.

REVIEW

Unit 1

1 What school subject is it? Unscramble the letters.

a) EIHSLGN

___

b) THMA

___

c) YOIHSTR

___

d) EOAYHPRGG

___

e) ESGPOTUUER

___

f) ESCCNIE

___

g) TRA

___

h) LPAHCYIS OIAUEDCTN

___

2 Answer the question about yourself.

a) What is your favorite school subject?

___

b) Is there a school subject you don't like? Why?

___

3 Write A or AN before the following words.

a) _____ man · **e)** _____ house · **i)** _____ apple

b) _____ elephant · **f)** _____ ice cream cone · **j)** _____ athlete

c) _____ fish · **g)** _____ ball · **k)** _____ engineer

d) _____ airplane · **h)** _____ piano · **l)** _____ nurse

4 Complete with your school week timetable.

Monday	Tuesday	Wednesday	Thursday	Friday

5 Which is the correct preposition? Use the ones from the box.

in • in front of • between • on

a) _____ · **b)** _____

Unit 2

1 Look at the pictures and name the sports.

2 If your special day at school would have American sports, what sports in activity 1 would you choose?

3 What sports do they practice? Write the answer.

swimming * basketball * tennis * volleyball
running * soccer * karate * cycling

Unit 3

1 Match the activities with the pictures.

a) To cook

b) To eat

c) To talk

d) To watch a movie

e) To play

2 Read the instructions and draw the picture. Pay attention to the use of *this, those* and *these.*

In this picture:
- A boy is standing in his bedroom.
- This is his chair.
- Those are his books.
- These are his games.

Unit 4

1 Match the items with the images on the menu. What would you like to have?

a) fr ed chicken

b) hot dog

c) juice

d) hamburger

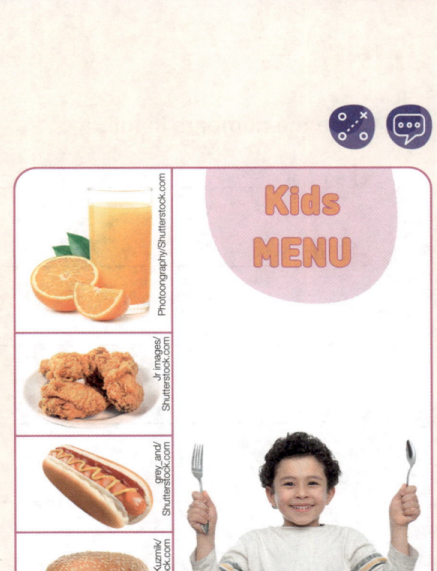

2 Organize the food in the correct box.

french fries • apple • water • soda
ice cream • meat • chicken • lettuce

Healthy food	**Junk food**
_____	_____
_____	_____
_____	_____
_____	_____

Unit 5

1 Write the numbers in full.

a) 19 _____

b) 25 _____

c) 36 _____

d) 62 _____

e) 77 _____

f) 100 _____

Complete the questions with **what, where, when, why** or **who**.

a) _____ do you live?

— I live in São Paulo.

b) _____ is your best friend?

— My best friend is Paola.

c) _____ do you do in your free time?

— I read and play video games in my free time.

d) _____ do you like to read?

— I like to read because it's fun.

e) _____ do you have Math class?

— On Mondays.

Unit 6

 Complete with the verb **to be: am, is,** or **are.**

a) I _____ sleepy. **e)** Bill _____ a lawyer.

b) She _____ my teacher. **f)** He _____ a musician.

c) We _____ friends. **g)** I _____ a dentist.

d) You _____ tall. **h)** We _____ teachers.

 Complete the sentences with the correct form of the verb **to be.**

a) Thomas _____ my best friend.

b) Liz and Tim _____ in the Physical Education class.

c) We _____ close to the department store.

d) Grace _____ a wonderful wheelchair basketball player.

3 Match the parts of these musical instruments. Write their names.

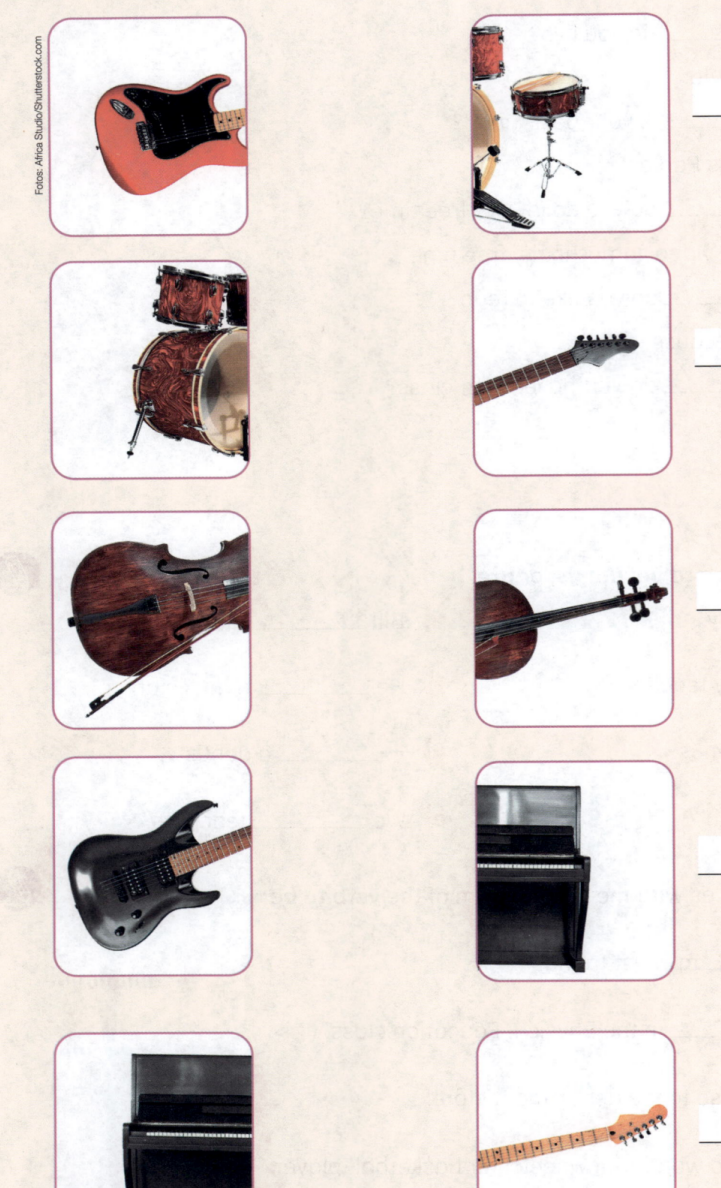

Unit 7

1 Complete the crossword with the correct clothing item.

2 What places are they? Write them down.

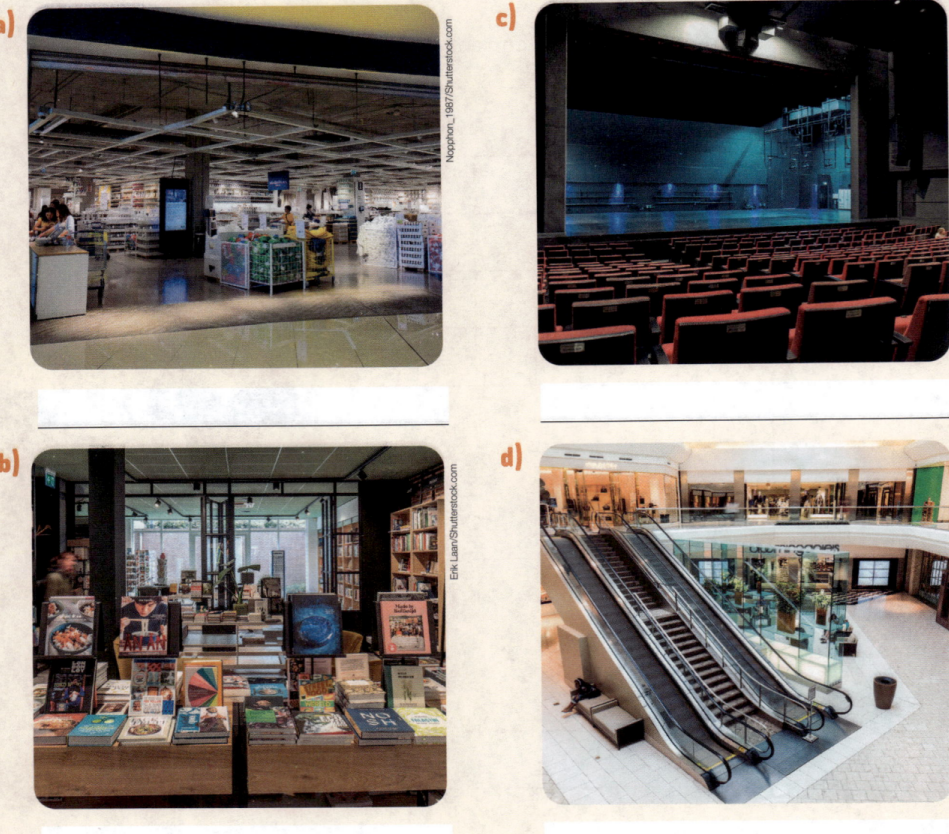

3 What are they wearing? Look and write.

Unit 8

1 Complete the sequence of ordinal numbers.

a) _____ – first · · · · · · **d)** _____ – fourth

b) _____ – second · · · · · · **e)** _____ – fifth

c) _____ – third

2 Complete the ordinal numbers. Then, write how many people there are in each picture and their profession. Follow the example.

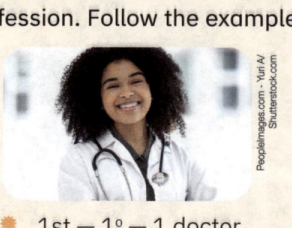

- $1st - 1º - 1$ doctor

a)

_____nd — _____ — _____

b)

_____rd — _____ — _____

3 What job is it? Unscramble the letters.

a) LIPTO · · · · · · **d)** UIMANSCI

_____ · · · · · · _____

b) CAMHNEIC · · · · · · **e)** DJEGU

_____ · · · · · · _____

c) SOLUJNITAR

_____

4 Help the police officer catch the thief. Choose the correct path.

GLOSSARY

A

A lot of: muito(a)/(os)/(as)
About: sobre
Across: através (de)
Again: novamente, de novo
All of a sudden: de repente
All the time: o tempo todo
American football: futebol americano
American Museum of Natural History: Museu Americano de História Natural
Anytime: a qualquer hora, toda vez, quando quiser
Arrive, to: chegar

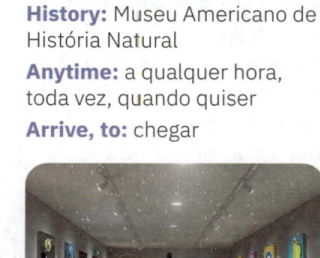

Art: Arte
Aspiring: aspirante, ambicioso
Awesome: ncrível

B

Backpack: mochila
Bait: isca
Bake, to: assar
Baker: padeiro(a)
Baseball: beisebol
Basketball: basquetebol
Bass: baixo

Beans: feijão
Beginning: começo
Behave, to: comportar-se
Bell: sino
Belong, to: pertencer
Between: entre
Biggest: maior
Blithe: jovial, alegre
Blow, to: soprar
Body: corpo

Bookshelf: estante
Bookstore: livraria
Both: ambos
Boyfriend: namorado
Brag, to: vangloriar-se
Bread: pão
Breakfast: café da manhã
Build, to: construir
Burn, to: queimar
Bush: arbusto
Busy: ocupado(a)/(os)/(as)
Butter: manteiga
Buy, to: comprar

C

Cake: bolo
Calendar: calendário, agenda
Call out, to: gritar

Care, to: se importar
Cart: carrinho
Catch, to: pegar
Cereal: cereal
Challenge, to: desafiar
Character: personagem
Cheese: queijo

Chef: chefe de cozinha/ cozinheiro(a) profissional
Chemist: químico(a) (profissão)
Chicken: frango
Child: criança
Chocolate: chocolate
Class: aula
Classical: clássico(a)
Clean: limpo(a)/(as)/(os)
Clothes: roupas
Coffee: café
Come, to: vir
Come on in: entre
Companionship: companhia
Consumerism: consumismo
Cookie: biscoito
Count, to: contar
Country: gênero de música surgido nos Estados Unidos, ligado aos trabalhadores e ao campo. Similar ao gênero musical brasileiro sertanejo
Crispy: crocante

Crowd: torcida, multidão
Cycling: ciclismo

D

Daily: diariamente
Department store: loja de departamentos
Dinner: jantar
Disability: deficiência
Doctor: médico

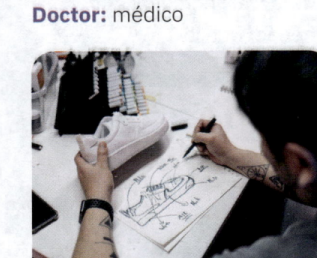

Draw, to: desenhar
Dress up, to: vestir-se
Drink, to: beber

E

Each: cada

Ear: orelha
Easter: Páscoa
Egg: ovo
Emperor: imperador
Enemy: inimigo
Engineer: engenheiro(a)

English: inglês
Enough: suficiente
Evolve, to: evoluir
Excited for: animado(a) para

F

Fable: fábula
Fall: outono
Fan: ventilador
Far away/far from: longe, distante
Favorite: favorito(a)
Fashionable: na moda
Field trip: excursão escolar
Firefighter: bombeiro(a)
Fish: peixe
Flip, to: virar
Flip-flops: chinelo
Float, to: flutuar
Flute: flauta
Fly, to: voar
Follow, to: seguir
Food: comida
Food court: praça de alimentação
Football games: jogos de futebol americano
Foreign: estrangeiro(a)
Fossil: fóssil
French fries: batatas fritas
Fret, to: incomodar
Friend: amigo(a)

Friendship: amizade

Fruit: fruta
Frying pan: frigideira
Fun: diversão
Future: futuro

G

Game: jogo, partida
Gather, to: reunir-se
Genre: gênero
Geography: Geografia
Get back, to: voltar
Get rid of, to: livrar-se de
Go shopping, to: ir às compras
Gold: ouro, dourado(a)
Grains: grãos
Green cross code: código cruzado verde
Grow up, to: crescer
Guitar: violão, guitarra
Guys: turma, pessoal

Gymnastics: ginástica

H

Ham: presunto
Hamburger: hambúrguer

H

Hare: lebre
Health: saúde
Healthy: saudável
Hear, to: ouvir
Heavy: pesado(a)
Help, to: ajudar
Hide, to: esconder
Historical: histórico
History: História
Hot dog: cachorro-quente
How good: quão bom
How long: por quanto tempo

I

Ice cream: sorvete
In front of: na frente de
Interest: interesse
Interesting: interessante
Invisible: invisível
Isle: ilha

J

Janitor: zelador(a)
Jeans: *jeans*
Job: emprego, profissão
Journalist: jornalista

Judge: juiz, juíza
Juice: suco
Junk food: alimento não saudável

K

Karate: caratê
Keep, to: manter
Kitchen: cozinha

Kite: pipa
Know, to: saber

L

Labor: trabalho
Lawyer: advogado(a)
Leap year: ano bissexto
Learn, to: aprender
Let me see: deixe-me ver
Let's go: vamos

Lettuce: alface
Lovely: adorável
Lunch: almoço

M

Make, to: fazer
Make fun of, to: tirar sarro de
Mall: *shopping center*
Mate: colega
Math: Matemática
Mayor: prefeito
Meal: refeição

Mechanic: mecânico(a)
Menu: cardápio
Merry: feliz
Messy: bagunceiro(a)
Milk: leite
Mingle, to: misturar-se
Mistake: erro
Most: mais
Movies: cinema, filmes
Much: muito
Museum: museu
Musician: músico
My favorite: meu/minha favorito(a)

N

Naked: nu(a)

Nap: cochilo
Natural: natural
Near: perto
Never: nunca
New: novo(a)
Next: próximo(a)
Nicely: bem
Nurse: enfermeiro(a)

O

Once upon a time: era uma vez
Order: pedido
Out of sight: longe dos olhos

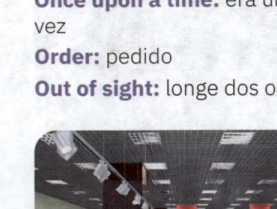

Outlet: loja de ponta de estoque
Outrageously: escandalosamente
Outside: fora
Over there: ali
Ownership: posse

P

Pants: calça
Parasports: para-esportes
Parents: pais
Pasta: macarrão
Pay close attention, to: preste bastante atenção
Peanut: amendoim
Pencil case: estojo
Penny: centavo
People: pessoas
Percussion: percussão
Photographer: fotográfo(a)
Physical Education: Educação Física
Picture: figura, imagem
Pilot: piloto
Piper: flautista
Place: lugar
Play, to: tocar
Playmate: colega de brincadeira
Plod, to: andar devagar, fazer algo com calma
Police officer: policial
Polite: formal
Popsicle: picolé
Portuguese: Português

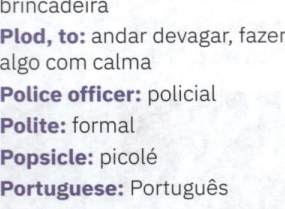

Postman: carteiro
Pout, to: fazer cara feia
Precious: precioso(a)
Price: preço
Profession: profissão

Professional: profissional
Put, to: colocar
Put out, to: apagar

R

Railroad: trilhos, estrada de ferro
Railway: estrada de ferro
Remember, to: lembrar
Request: pedido
Reward: recompensa, prêmio
Rice: arroz
Root for, to: torcer para/por
Rover: andarilho, pirata
Rule: regra
Running: corrida

S

Sandal: sandália
Sandwich: sanduíche
Saxophone: saxofone
Say, to: dizer
Seem, to: parecer
Several: diversos, vários
Schedule: agenda, programação
Science: Ciências
Scientific and cultural institution: instituição científica e cultural

Sculpture: escultura
Shaker: chocalho
Shame: vergonha
Shelf: prateleira
Shirt: camisa
Shoe: sapato
Shorts: bermuda
Shout, to: gritar
Show off, to: gabar-se
Sick: doente
Silver: prata, prateado(a)
Singer: cantor(a)
Sink, to: afundar
Skirt: saia
Snack: petisco
Snack bar: lanchonete
Sneakers: tênis
Soccer: futebol
Sock: meia
Soda: refrigerante
Solve, to: resolver
Someone: alguém
Soon: em breve, logo
Sound, to: soar
Soundtrack: trilha sonora
Spend, to: gastar
Sport: esporte
Spring: primavera

Sprinkle, to: polvilhar
Stadium: estádio
Stand, to: permanecer
Statue: estátua
Steak: bife
Store: loja
Stranger: desconhecido(a), forasteiro
String: corda
Student: aluno(a)
Subject: assunto, matéria
Sugar: açúcar
Suit: traje, terno
Summer: verão
Super Bowl: Super Bowl – final do campeonato de futebol americano
Sustainable shopping: compras sustentáveis
Stupid: estúpido, bobo
Sweetie: querido(a)
Swimming: natação
Synonym: sinônimo

T

Tailor: alfaiate
Take, to: tomar
Take away, to: levar embora
Take someone out, to: levar alguém para passear
Tambourine: pandeiro
Tea: chá
Teacher: professor(a)
Team: time
Tennis: tênis (esporte)
Theater: teatro
Thief: ladrão

Think: pensar
Those are: estes são
Time: tempo
Tiring: cansativo(a)
Tomato: tomate
Tortoise: tartaruga
Touchdown: pontuação do futebol americano
Trade: comércio

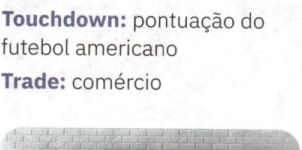

Trash bin: lixeira
Treasure: tesouro
Treat, to: tratar, cuidar
T-shirt: camiseta
Type: tipo

U

Ugly: feio(a)
Underground: subterrâneo(a)

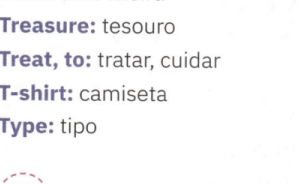

Underwear: roupa íntima
Unscramble, to: desembaralhar
Use, to: utilizar

V

Vegetables: legumes
Vegetable salad: salada de legumes
Very: muito
Veterinarian: veterinário(a)
Violin: violino
Volleyball: voleibol

W

Wait, to: esperar
Waitress: garçonete
Warm, to: aquecer

Wastebasket: lixeira
Watch, to: assistir
Water: água

Wave: onda
Wear: vestir
Week: semana
Weekly: semanalmente
Welcome: bem-vindo(a), boas-vindas
West: oeste
What's up: E aí?
Wheelchair: cadeira de rodas
Win, to: vencer
Wind: sopro, vento

Winter: inverno
Wood block: bloco de madeira
Work: trabalho
World: mundo
Would be: seria
Would like: gostaria

Y

Year: ano
Young: jovem
You'd like: você gostaria

Z

Zest: entusiasmo

INDEX

SONGS

UNIT 1	Work and play		**24**
UNIT 2	Take me out to the ball game		**34**
UNIT 3	Make new friends		**47**
UNIT 4	Five crispy pancakes		**56**
UNIT 5	Calendar song		**72**
UNIT 6	Music man		**80**
UNIT 7	One, two, let's buy my shoe		**95**
UNIT 8	I love working on the railroad		**104**

LISTENINGS

UNIT 1

A special school day ———————— **17**
Prepositions of place ———————— **22**
School subjects ———————— **27**

UNIT 2

Sports and health ———————— **29**
Possessive pronouns ———————— **33**
Wheelchair basketball match ———————— **36**

UNIT 3

A friend's visit ———————— **39**
Julia's pencil case ———————— **49**

UNIT 4

At the cafeteria ———————— **51**
Ordering food in a restaurant ———————— **58**
Healthy food and junk food ———————— **60**

UNIT 5

The fun visit to the museum ———————— **63**
Museum visit chart ———————— **70**
Class field trip ———————— **71**

UNIT 6

The Music class ———————— **75**
Musical instruments ———————— **82**
Music genres ———————— **84**

UNIT 7

At the shopping mall ———————— **89**
Tim and Thomas at the mall ———————— **96**

UNIT 8

Different jobs ———————— **99**
Cardinal and ordinal numbers ———————— **106**
What do you want to be? ———————— **106**

CELEBRATIONS

Valentine's day

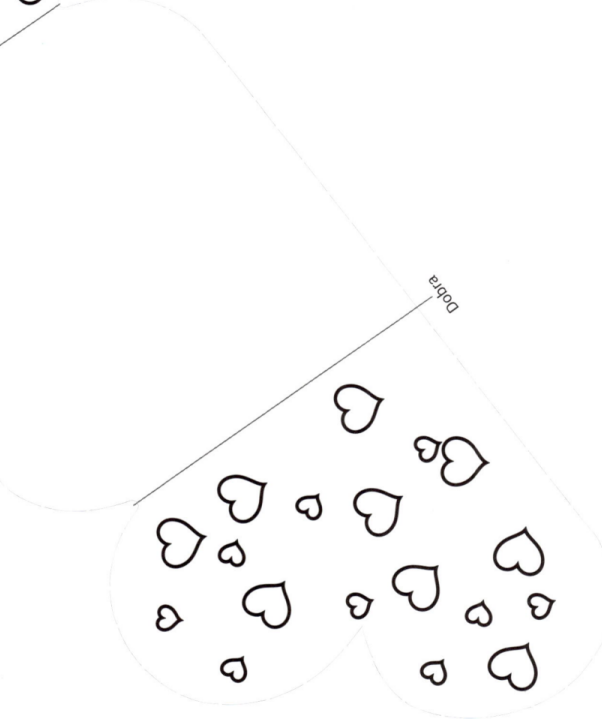

Carnival

Carnival

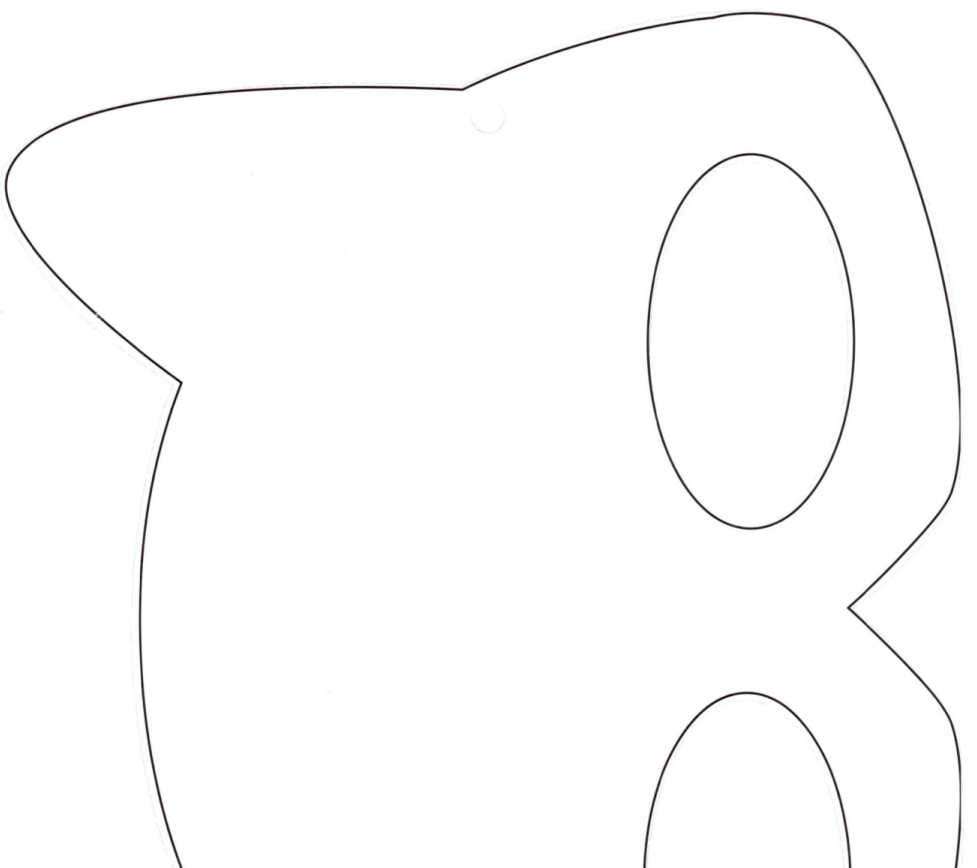

Easter

Easter

International Family's day

Dobra

World Music Day

	**Violin**		**Saxophone**
	**Piano**		**Clarinet**
	**Banjo**		**Harmonica**
	**Drums**		**Keyboard**
	**Shakers**		**Accordion**
	**Trumpet**		**Guitar**

Christmas

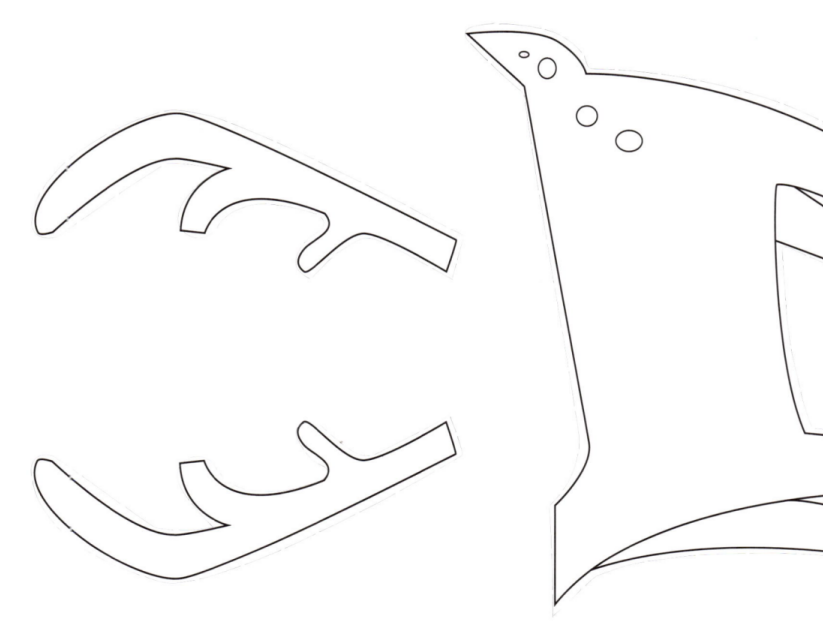

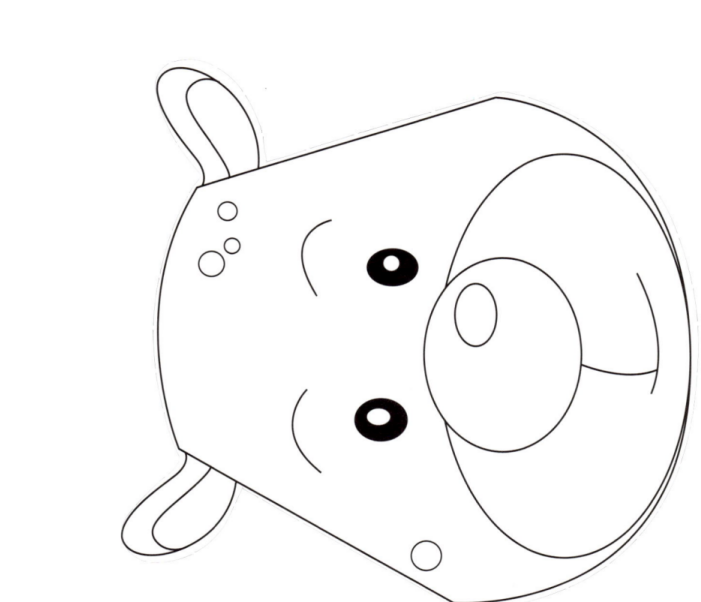

STICKERS

Let's start!

Page 15

Unit 1

Page 28

STICKERS

Unit 2

Page 30

Unit 3

Page 50

STICKERS

Unit 4

Page 60

Unit 5

Page 64

STICKERS

Unit 6

Page 84

Unit 7

Page 98

Unit 8

Page 101